EverydayArt

For Kids

For Kids

Projects to
Unlock Creativity

Carolyn Holm

Mockingbird Press

Mockingbird Press
PO Box 331
El Cerrito, CA 94530
(510) 528-7804

Cover photography by Chriss Poulsen

ISBN 0-9648066-0-6

Library of Congress Catalog Card Number 95-95015

First Edition

Printed in the United States of America

10 9 8 7 6 5 4 3 2 1

This book is dedicated to my mother,
who never allowed coloring books.

Acknowledgements

I especially want to thank Sara Steck for her inspiration and support in getting this book started, and for her fountain of ideas, enthusiasm, and practical advice garnered from her classroom experience as an art teacher.

I want to thank my husband, Hratch Kouyoumdjian, who made this book possible, who puts up with a basement full of strange art supplies (many of which look suspiciously like trash), and was patient and supportive throughout the writing process.

I want to thank Mary Jo Starkey, Renee Guillory, and Jean Shell, all of whom took the time to carefully read drafts of this book, providing valuable advice and feedback. I want to thank Chriss Poulsen for putting his talent to work on the cover photo. I want to express my appreciation to Barbara and Michael Jonas for their always sage advice and thought-provoking critiques. And I am also grateful for all that I learned working with Ann Clements, and for inspiration and ideas from Bev Bos.

I want to thank my students and their parents, for their enthusiasm and support of art as an everyday joy, and for the inspirational way these students interpret my projects, time after time.

And finally, I want to thank my daughter, Lena, for her cheerful productivity, creative enthusiasm, and everyday passion for art.

Table of

❖

Contents

Art is not a special sauce
applied to ordinary cooking;
it is the cooking itself...

W. R. Lethaby

For Kids

Introduction

Art can be so many things...a way of expressing our identity, a way to see things in a new way, a way to communicate to and connect ourselves with our community, a way to celebrate grace and beauty, a way to communicate our deepest thoughts, a way to touch our spiritual core. Art can be profound...it can be decorative. But it should never be something left up on a pedestal, for a few to appreciate and fewer still to produce. Art should be an *everyday* thing.

When art is an everyday thing for children, they gain far more than just an aesthetic experience or an afternoon of fun: they discover problem solving skills; they build up self-reliance, self-motivation and self-esteem; they develop "fresh eyes" that let them see things in new ways; they are rewarded with the tangible results of concentration and good work habits; and, they get in the *habit of creative thinking*. And all of this, of course, transfers to every other part of their lives.

In *Everyday Art* you will find a wide range of projects, from painting, collage and sculpture, to clothing, toys and everyday objects...what they have in common is they nurture the habit of creativity. These are projects children can do at home...sometimes with help, sometimes with direction, but always on their own terms. They are presented simply as ideas...starting places to motivate a child to explore, rather than step-by-step blueprints that produce "look-alike" results. The emphasis is upon materials that are easily obtained, including recycled materials. With the simplest of materials you will find children will produce wonderfully imaginative creations!

The biggest relief for most parents will be that you do not have to be an artist yourself to create an environment that will truly nurture your child's creativity.   Your job as a parent is not to guide your child through the steps of a project. Your job is simply to provide the environment, the materials, the support and the appreciation.   In fact, you are a success if your child has been inspired to experiment, to create something *on his own*. This is more fun than you may imagine...you may find yourself sitting down next to your young artist and trying some of these projects yourself!

So turn off the tv...it's time to make art an *everyday experience!*

Carolyn Holm

Setting Up!

Providing a Creative Environment

*Until modern times,
apart from the esoteric knowledge
of the priests, philosophers and astronomers,
the greater part of human thought and
imagination flowed through the hands.*

Lewis Mumford

The Creativity Habit

We live in a world that will increasingly require creativity for success. We keep hearing that there will be less need for assembly line workers, and far more need for those who are creative enough to solve problems, see things in new ways, invent better ways to do things. And in an ever-changing world, people will need to be creative enough to continually retrain themselves in a rapidly evolving workplace.

At the same time, however, we find ourselves in a world in which everyday opportunities to be creative, to develop the creative *habit*, are diminishing. It used to be that people always made their own clothes, cooked everything "from scratch", and fashioned their own tools. They knew how things went together, so they could explore their own variations, and put their own personal stamp on them. When a problem came up, they applied what they knew and used their creative thinking to design the solution.

And while a privileged few had all this done for them, *everyone,* rich or poor, made their own entertainment. They didn't sit passively in front of an electronic screen... they whittled toys, stitched quilts, told stories, made up songs, played music. Life was not passive - it actively engaged the mind. Creativity - and the creative habit - was something that was developed in the process.

We find ourselves in a world in which everyday opportunities to be creative, to develop the creative habit, are diminishing.

5

This kind of creative exploration, unfettered by preconceptions and uninhibited by self-doubt, resides in every child at life's starting gate.

Such a habit - one of flexing an active, engaged and creative mind - is what we all want for our children.

But without a lifestyle that naturally develops the habit of being creative, we need to make a concerted effort to pursue it. We send our children to school, hoping they will acquire it there. When we can, we enrich their lives and after-school hours with books, library visits, community classes, music and cultural programs.

Fortunately, we each start out with a creative mind. Watch any preschooler take up a toy he's never seen before. In five minutes he'll put it to more uses than its adult designer ever dreamed of! This kind of creative exploration, unfettered by preconceptions and uninhibited by self-doubt, resides in every child at life's starting gate. But all too often it somehow gets lost, as if it were atrophied as a child grows older. If we can capture and nurture this creative potential, to reinforce the creativity of a child's early years, we can help them make it a lifelong habit. What a gift to give our children!

The Open Art Process

Art is one of the easiest vehicles for developing creativity in children. And along with creativity, there are other important benefits...self-reliance, self esteem, cognitive skills...this is why educators urge the incorporation of art into all kinds of children's academic study (*see quote at right.*)

All too often, though, art is put on a pedestal or treated as a frill that is separate from academic pursuits.

Most of us adults do not consider ourselves artists, or even artistic. Our lives are distant from the artistic process, so it is easy to regard art as something for the talented few... something that hangs in galleries and museums....something we read about in newspapers and magazines... something we frame and hang on our living room wall. This is adult art. Art with a capital A.

For those adults who *have* made art a part of their lives, no matter the ambition, no matter the scale, it has brought them joy and satisfaction. And what they have learned from the creative process transfers over to other parts of their lives.

*"**F**or all students, study of the arts can increase self-discipline and motivation, contribute to a positive self-image, provide an acceptable outlet for emotions, and help to develop creative and intuitive thinking processes not always inherent in other academic pursuits. In addition, for students who learn most effectively through nonverbal modes, the arts provide additional opportunities for successful learning experiences. Moreover, the arts can create a meaningful context for learning and can foster improved learning retention through multisensory approaches. The study of the arts can also contribute to the appreciation of historical and multicultural understandings and the development of problem-solving ability."*

From: *The Visual and Performing Arts Framework for California Public Schools: Kindergarten Through Grade Twelve,* © California Department of Education, 1989.

The process itself is more important than any adult-judged results... a process leading freely to multiple interpretations, various end results, and even unpredictable directions!

It is even more so for children. For them art is never a frill, not just aesthetics, or limited to pictures in a museum. It is not esoteric. It is not just for "talented" kids. It is a tool for exploring themselves, their world, and their part in it. It is communication and problem-solving. It is a form of play, and play is children's business, their way of learning how the world works. And it is a source of tremendous pride of accomplishment. Art should be an *everyday* thing.

Young children take to art like birds to the air. They do not need special talent - *they all have talent residing within them. Any* child can "turn on" to art. And *any* parent can nurture this process. A parent does not have to be "artistic" to provide an environment rich in creative potential. Neither does the parent have to be affluent. But the parent must provide materials and a supportive environment. And to provide a supportive environment, the parent should know the difference between Open Art and Closed Art.

What is Open Art?

Open Art is an art process that allows the child to explore an art project on his own, uninhibited by outside expectations. It is a process that tends to lead to multiple interpretations, various end results, and even unpredictable directions. It is a process that thrives in a non-critical environment, in which the child's exploration is allowed to proceed without adult interference or correction. It is a process in which the *process itself* is more important than any adult-judged results.

The result? It may be strange, or beautiful, or charming, or may not even look like much to the adult eye. But it will be the child's *own product*, and what the child gets from this process is priceless.

What is Closed Art?

We've all seen it. The bulletin board displaying a group's art project, each piece virtually identical. The similarity of the work is a result of a process in which the children are shown *what* they are going to do, shown *how*

to do it, and often assisted in the process. The *measure* of its success is its close resemblance to the sample shown at the beginning of the process.

There may be some benefit to such a project. Small motor development, in some cases. Patterning practice, in others. Certainly it is an exercise in following directions. But it isn't using any creativity. The children are not solving any problems. They can't really say they did it by themselves. And they may even be self-critical of their ability to recreate what their leader has shown them.

You guessed it. They have been participating in a closed art process.

In contrast, an Open Art approach would have been for the adult to provide the materials, provide a goal, and if necessary, initiate some discussion in order to provide direction. If a child wanted help, the adult would introduce helpful skills and techniques, but then would stand back to allow the children to learn and use these skills and techniques on their own. As they tackle the project, the children would have been allowed to explore the medium as they worked with it, completing the project with any variations they may have conjured up. *And the results would not look alike.*

In a Closed Art project, the measure of its success is its close resemblance to the sample shown at the beginning of the process.

9

The Seven Benefits of an Open Art Process

Problem Solving
Discovering just what actually works...learning to rely upon oneself to find solutions...
exploring new experiences without inhibition.

◆

Fresh Eyes
Learning to see things in new ways.

◆

Skills Practice
Using academic learning skills, such as measuring, estimating, and patterning...
developing and honing small motor skills.

◆

Concentration & Good Work Habits
Being in control is a motivation for taking greater care to do it well...and like magic,
this care rewards the effort.

◆

Freedom from Right and Wrong
The reassurance that risk can freely be taken because there simply is no
truly right or wrong way to do art.

◆

Self-reliance
The heady sense of power and confidence that comes with doing things
without someone else's control...*all by yourself.*

◆

Self-esteem
The true pride of accomplishment, of problems overcome.

Creating an Open Art Environment

In order for Open Art to flourish you must create the right environment. Of course you need the physical environment...the work area. But the emotional environment, how the parent responds to the art, is the one that may take the most thought.

After all, for most of us, parenting is very much on-the-job training, and few of us are prepared for the subtleties of what to say and what not to say to a budding artist. We mean well, but we fall into all kinds of pitfalls, simply because of our adult point of view.

Open art is more about the *process* than about the result. But we adults are in the habit of focusing our attention on results. We are *judged* by our results, *paid* for our results, *identified* by our results. Do you think anyone would call you a writer if you have never been published? Not in the adult world.

As adults working with children, we need to be cautious about our habit of being concerned with results. We can all too easily fall into the trap of putting adult expectations on children's products.

One trap is the reality trap. This occurs when we put tremendous value on a picture that looks "realistic".

Art does not have to follow the same "rules" that we expect of our eyesight!

But isn't it important for a picture to look real?

We adults expect to see reality. And we are so sure that we know reality when we see it. Or as we believe we see it with our eyes. The sun is yellow, the grass is green. We need to be reminded that on occasion the sun can be red, the grass yellow. It depends. Sometimes it takes an artist to show us that the mood may be better served with a green sun, purple grass. While young children can be much more flexible about "reality", they take their cues from the adults around them. So we adults sometimes have to remind ourselves not to be so attached to that which looks "real". Art doesn't have to follow the same "rules" that we expect of our eyesight!

What if I can't tell what the picture is about?

Adult expectations often require that a picture *be* of something. We forget about all the abstracts hanging in museums, and say to our children "What is that?". But it doesn't have to be anything at all. It can simply express the delight of color, of texture, of wet paint, of interesting objects stuck together.

All too often the same adult expectations forget to take into account the development level of a child. We need to remember that kids' art *looks like* kids' art. It does not look like grown up illustrations, or grown up craft projects. When we forget this, we find ourselves comparing kids art to adult art.

Open art is not about kids copying an adult model. It is not about following the pattern dictated by someone else. It is not about coloring in someone else's picture.

Coloring books, forms and molds for clay and play dough, ready-made templates and stencils, rubber stamps...these are all closed art forms, in themselves, that allow children to mimic adult technique. They are not necessarily harmful, and in fact some can be delightful art tools. But as a steady diet from an early age, they are just "empty calories". They do not encourage creativity, problem-solving or self-sufficiency.

Adult expectations that compare children's art to adult art can also prevent us from truly appreciating what a child has created. "*It doesn't look like an elephant*" a well meaning adult may say doubtfully about a young child's picture. But this picture may have all the important elements of an elephant...prominent ears and nose, a skinny tail, and long stumpy legs. It may be the very *essence of elephantness*. It's only in our adult minds that these features do not actually add up to a proper elephant! But our words discourage a child who may have accomplished a very sophisticated drawing for her developmental level.

Sadder still is when an adult, just as well meaning, steps in and says "*That doesn't look like an elephant. Here, let me help you.*" The implied message is that the child is hopeless, she'll never get it without your help! We would never *intentionally* say this explicitly to a child, but over and over this message is given to children. How many of you reading this book learned early on that you were not good at art? You got one of those messages. And you probably gave up trying.

Take Coloring Books...

Coloring books simply have no place in the creative process. Why encourage a passive coloring activity (that ultimately becomes boring) instead of active drawing from the imagination? If it is so important for a child to learn to color neatly between the lines, let her draw her own picture, her *own* lines, and then color those in.

But coloring books are even worse than passive. They actually can inhibit the creative process by imposing an adult standard of draftsmanship, setting kids up for frustration with their own level of ability. Meanwhile, this standard also feeds the myth that you have to be a "good drawer" to be "artistic". (You don't. There are many forms of art that are not dependent upon realistic rendering.)

For the price of a coloring book, you can get a pad of blank paper, and make a far more useful contribution to a child's education.

13

When
we try to help
our children by
doing things
for them, our
underlying
message is that
they are not
capable of
doing it
themselves...
we are robbing
them of both a
learning
opportunity
and a step
towards self-
reliance.

Shouldn't I help my child?

A hands-off approach by the adult is a way of treating the child's artwork with respect. An adult should not change it, edit it, even *touch* it without the child's permission. When a group of children are doing art together, the young child who cannot yet write her name should be asked *if*, and *where*, she wants her name written on her art. Otherwise it should be unobtrusively written on the back of the artwork.

By putting a value on what he has done all by himself you are putting a value on that child. You are saying that he is special. When we try to help our children by doing things for them, our underlying message is that they are not capable of doing it themselves. By stepping in and taking it away from them, we are robbing them of both a learning opportunity and a step towards self-reliance. The child will learn self-reliance only by taking his *own* risks, learning from his own mistakes and failures, and overcoming these to discover success.

When we *allow* our child to try things, to take her own risks, our message is that we believe she is capable of learning by herself, whether by failure or by success. And when she is finally successful, she can truly enjoy the heady flush of self-sufficiency and the pride of real accomplishment.

What if she asks me to help her?

Children *will* ask for help. Some are even in the *habit* of allowing someone else to solve their problems for them. In order to encourage independence and problem solving habits, the parent needs to be aware that while sometimes the child really does need a hand, much of the time they can be guided through the situation so that they learn to handle it themselves.

The child who asks for help cutting out a picture may need smaller scissors. She may need to be shown how to cut the item from the page with a large margin, and then to go back in and cut the details. If she is too young to be able to cut out details, then cutting with a margin is good enough. To cut for her is to take away this learning experience, and to cut it for her because she cannot do the details is missing the point of doing art in the first place. Producing a detailed cutout may please an adult, but is never so important that a child should have it taken out of her hands so it can be "done right".

The child who wants to be *shown* how to do something needs to be encouraged to try it on his own. If he stares at his new watercolors and worries "*What do I DO with these?*" provide him with a sheet of paper just for experimentation and discovery. Ask him what kind of marks the different kinds of brushes make, and he will tentatively give it a try. Once he is engaged with the material, the experimentation will build upon itself...soon he will forget he ever wondered what to do.

The child who does NOT want any help, but who is frustrated by something he finds difficult, may just need a suggestion to get on the right track. If you think a technique or material might make it easier for him to accomplish what he wants to do, ask him if he would like you to show him something he may want to try. Then it is up to him to implement this information.

Finally, the child who is always concerned that she is "making mistakes" may need to be quoted the one golden rule in art, that *there are no mistakes, just a change of plans.* It's always interesting to see what children come up with when they learn to explore and make something else out of their "mistakes".

What if he is doing it wrong?

In this context, there really are no right or wrong ways to do something. There may be safety concerns that have a definite right way and wrong way, and there may be issues about house-destroying messes that must be dealt with, but when it comes to exploring a medium, right and wrong become a moot point. If a young child refuses to

Producing a detailed cutout may please an adult, but it is never so important that a child should have it taken out of her hands so it can be "done right".

The one golden rule of art: there are no mistakes, just a change of plans.

15

hold a brush "correctly", or prefers to use her elbow instead of a brush, there is no reason to stop her. If your older child wants to experiment with pictures using charcoal mixed with turpentine and linseed oil, let him (but you may want to issue a warning about fingerprints on the woodwork.)

Are there any parameters at all?

Parameters that are simply structure for the art process, that do not limit execution, are in fact very useful. Setting some guidelines in a project can create a challenge that inspires children to do something that they would not otherwise have tried. But once those parameters have been established, there should be no control on the child's attempt to deal with them.

An example of a good parameter? Suggest your child do a painting that is completely abstract. Or one using only black and two other colors. This creates an interesting challenge. But remember, bite your tongue and refrain from saying "*those don't go together*" when your child chooses two colors that *you* don't like together!

Is it OK to have rules?

In most households, tension mounts when projects start making the house a mess. In fact, the inevitable mess involved is one of the biggest deterrents to doing art projects at home. But clear ground rules from the start make the mess manageable.

Kids are used to clean-up at school at the end of a project. There is no reason the same clean-up rule should not apply at home. If you stick to it, clean-up will finally become part of the project. In fact, you get to be the one to remind everyone "*The project isn't done until it is cleaned up*" (and one day your child will grow up, find herself saying that to *her* children, and will agonize "*I've turned into my Mom!*")

Remember to be specific during the cleanup process. Younger children are rendered paralyzed by any order that is as general and vague as "*Clean this stuff up.*"

Setting guidelines can create the kinds of challenge that inspires children to do something that they would not otherwise have tried.

16

On the other hand, they spring into action when given a specific command such as "*Pick up all the scraps of paper and put them into the waste basket.*" Your job is to issue a series of orders just as specific until the area is clean and all materials put away. This tedium will continue until they are old enough to know what to do unprompted. (That day will come.)

You will want to have an easy storage system so children can put away materials unassisted. You will also want a designated place for finished art. Proper care of finished work (and of materials) is a form of respect, and this respect should get its start at an early age.

From the beginning you will want to establish rules about the location of the work itself. For example, colored pencils create little mess, and may be considered a movable project, but paint, markers and crayons can ruin a rug, so you may want a clear rule that limits most projects to the "art area". If you have exceptions, like the colored pencils, be very specific about them.

Finally, you will need to have safety rules. There will be some tools and materials that are off-limits because they simply are not safe. And some tools will have rules for their use. For example, children should be taught not to run with scissors.

Speaking of off-limits, a child who has something very special - a technical pen, or a fine set of pastels - should be allowed to make it off-limits to siblings. Some tools simply are not to be shared.

***K**ids are used to clean-up at school at the end of a project. There is no reason the same clean-up rule should not apply at home.*

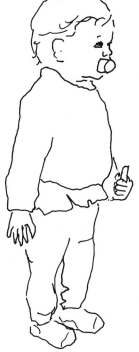

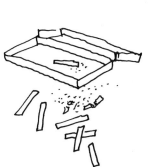

17

*B*elieve
it or not,
we should not
praise
everything
our child
produces.

What's the best thing to say when presented with a new piece of art?

As a proud parent, one of the toughest things to remember is that we should not praise everything our child produces. We need to learn to refrain from gushing. This is tough because it's so hard *not* to gush. When you see some of the strange and wonderful things that kids make, it is natural to exclaim "*Oh, I LOVE it!!!*". If you are a gusher, and most of us are, you need to take a second look at this habit. There are some side effects we do not intend!

Gushing "*Oh I LOVE it!!!*" makes your approval conditional. You are saying that you like *that* particular kind of art, which is of course a signal to make more like it. And what if you don't particularly like it? Then the absence of gush immediately becomes painfully apparent. And if you gush all the time, pretty soon the child, nobody's fool, dismisses your judgment. Have you ever heard "*Oh, Mom likes it, but Mom likes everything*"?

If you've heard that, then perhaps you have noticed that contrary to conventional wisdom, gushing compliments does not instill self-esteem. Taking risks (especially risking failure), learning from one's mistakes, discovering abilities, and forging success...these are *real* self-esteem builders.

Another seemingly innocent question is "*What is it*?" If you say this, chances are your child will scramble to come up with an It, even if the piece was completely abstract when he did it. *But it doesn't have to be anything at all.* He may have been enjoying the juxtaposition of certain colors, or the texture of paint, or the spatter made by banging the brush.

What *can* you say? You can be positive about the art by showing appreciation for the effort while remaining neutral about the result (*see "Best to Say" on the next page*). Better yet, you can become a silent observer. Non-judgmental, non-committal, you allow the child to tell you how *he* feels about his art.

And of course, by providing the materials and environment, and by proudly displaying his work, you are making the best possible comment of all.

Best to Say...

Sometimes the best environment for Open Art can be created when you bite your tongue! But as that is not always practical, here are some things you can say instead, when you feel the urge to gush:

"Tell me about this picture."

◆

"I like the way you figured how to do this all by yourself."

◆

"Which one of these is your favorite?"

◆

"I can see you really spent some careful time on this."

◆

"I like the way you used your colors."

◆

"I can see you really used your eyes when you drew this. You have so many good details here."

◆

"What a vibrant blue you've got here!"

The Physical Environment

By now it should be clear that *you the parent* do not have to be an *artist* to create an environment that is conducive to creative artwork. In fact, when your children have become habitual artists, you will be surprised to find that you have less and less to do with the process. Your role will become one of a materials provider, and on occasion, a suggestion bank.

But at the onset you will need to create the physical environment that encourages your child to spend time "doing art". It will be up to you to see that there is the time, the place, and the materials to support the creative effort.

*W*hen your children have become habitual artists you will find that you have less and less to do with the process.

Time

You do need to ensure that your child has some quiet unscheduled time for doing art. Our children's lives are filled with soccer practice, piano lessons, choir practice, baseball clinic, Girl Scout cookie sales, Cub Scout meetings, ballet, karate, homework...there is precious little time that is free. We need to keep some check on all these activities to make sure our children have blocks of unstructured time. And one of the things they will enjoy doing in the unstructured time is noodling around with art.

The Art Area

You will want to designate a good place for art projects. Ideally it will be comfortable, quiet, safe, invulnerable to reasonable messes, and out of reach of curious younger siblings.

Younger children especially will want to work near you, the parent. Don't expect a five year old to be very enthusiastic about doing art all by himself in his own room. By setting up an art area near *your* work area you will really be encouraging art activity. You will both be working side-by-side.   For this reason kitchen tables are probably the most frequent sites for art projects.

Older children, on the other hand, especially pre-teens and teens, will want to work in their rooms with the door firmly closed. (By starting them at a young age working near you, they will have developed the creativity habit by the time they are older, and will truly enjoy it in the privacy of their own rooms.)   A plastic drop cloth on the floor under the desk or work table is a good way to protect the bedroom floor.

The living room is usually not a good location, because art can be hard on a carpet. You need to face the fact that there will be a mess to some degree, whether it be from simple paper cuttings to great glops of paint accidentally flying across the room.

This mess can be a tragedy or barely an issue, depending upon how you prepare for it. A vinyl table cloth and an old tray are likely to be the two accessories that make art at home a pleasure rather than a chore.

Designate the tray for working with paste or glue, for small painting jobs, and for working with tiny materials that would spell disaster if spilled (beads, for instance). The tray will contain the mess. It also makes moving the project easier, especially when the activity is unfinished when it is time to clean up the table for dinner.

The tablecloth will protect your table from the vicissitudes of medium sized projects. For larger messy projects, you can put the tablecloth on the floor. The tray

A vinyl tablecloth and an old tray are likely to be the two accessories that make art projects at home a pleasure rather than a chore.

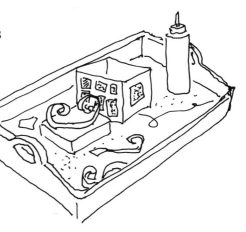

and the tablecloth should be *readily accessible to the child* so that art projects can be undertaken independently.

You will also want to have a "dedicated" sponge in a plastic container with the art materials. This is a sponge that will be used only for cleaning up art spills, so you will not want it to be the same sponge you use in your food preparation area. If everyone gets in the habit of wetting the sponge at the time that the project is being set up, it will be ready for use when a spill occurs.

Aprons are another good habit. They too should be kept handy, with the art supplies. Adult T-shirts make good art smocks for most kids. Get out those colorful vacation T-shirts that seemed so appropriate at the time - they'll finally be worn!

Storage

The next consideration is how to keep art materials both available and neat. Materials have a tendency to spill out everywhere. When they do they run the risk of getting stepped on, spilled on, chewed by a puppy, or shredded by a toddler. And the clutter of unruly materials is bad public relations for art activities.

A cupboard or book shelf can hold a group of plastic containers. You should have a place for paper, a container for collage materials, and ideally a plastic tote container for crayons, markers, scissors, glue, stapler, tape and pencil sharpener. Another tote could contain paints, brushes, paper towels, and water cups. All of these things should be easily reached by the child without your help, to encourage independence.

The materials that are collected for collage can be kept in plastic bins. As you accumulate these things you may want to sort them...natural materials, fabric scraps, patterned papers and pictures, and little "stuff" like corks, lids, small bottles...

Another storage problem is what to do with artwork when it is completed. This is a thorny issue. Of course we would like to display everything our children ever make, *forever*. But who has the space! So we compromise.

Designate a place for completed art to be stacked up after it is displayed. A large flat box under a bed is one solution. Date the work on the back, and if you have more than one child, make sure there is a name on it too.

Let the artwork pile up, and then periodically cull it. Save the very special pieces (some people take pictures of them) and, yes, discard the rest. There...it has been said. You have permission to discard some of your child's artwork. But most people recommend that you never let them see you do it!

Display

We all have refrigerators covered with artwork. But *do* go beyond this. Another display idea is to use plastic box frames, which are inexpensive and easily opened to change their contents. Special pieces should be permanently framed. *Do* frame some of your child's work and hang it in your home. It not only validates and honors your child's efforts, but you will be pleasantly surprised at how it looks! Even inexpensive dime store frames make a child's work of art look like gallery material!

Do frame some of your child's work and hang it in your home. It not only validates and honors your child's efforts, but you will be pleasantly surprised at how it looks!

Art and Beyond

In this book you may think that the usual definitions of art are being stretched a bit. Of course there are the projects we usually associate with Art - painting and drawing, sculpture, and lots of collage. But the projects also include making toys, making costumes, decorating backpacks, stringing beads. Is this art?

But does it have to hang in a gallery to be art? What about the art we wear? The handmade jewelry, the embroidered coat? What about the personal artifacts that surround us? The hand carved box? The hand stitched quilt? Yes, these too are art.

Children can have their introduction to these kinds of art by being encouraged to exercise their creativity every day, making all kinds of things. They can be encouraged to make their own games, their own toys, their own doll clothes. Older children can be encouraged to make their own unique clothes. In fact, art can be a wonderful way for pre-teens and teenagers to do what they so urgently need to do - express their newly discovered identities - on their backpacks, T-shirts, and room decorations.

But they won't do this unless they get started as young children, started in the *habit* of creativity.

And perhaps if they do, perhaps if we can help them get in the habit, not only of painting and drawing, but of *making all kinds of things* - their clothes, their jewelry, even their furnishings - in some small way we will be able to offset some of the rampant consumerism that surrounds and seduces them.

That is no small gift.

We can help our children get in the everyday habit of, not only painting and drawing, but making all kinds of things!

24

The Tools Around Us:

Materials, Media, Tools & Techniques

Every master knows
that the material teaches the artist.

Illya Ehrenburg

The Tools Around Us:
Materials, Media, Tools & Techniques

The cornerstone of any art program is the availability of good art materials. In fact, to an inventive mind, interesting art materials send the imagination soaring, inspiring countless new projects. The more experience a child has had experimenting with art materials and methods, the more she learns to be creative with them.

Materials come in all forms...from the precious single sheets of watercolor paper, so stiff, hefty and beautifully textured, to reams of thin gray newsprint...from softly colored pencils to rich oil paints...from paper mache to terra cotta clay...and from handmade papers to recycled household "stuff."

In this section you will find information about this wide variety of materials, grouped by type. Each tool or material is briefly described, with notes about age levels when appropriate. Scattered throughout this section are descriptions of some of the techniques involved.

This is a very brief, general overview, intended to help you get started. As your child matures, develops deeper interest in a medium, and wants to move on to a more sophisticated level, you will want to help him seek more information. By this time you will have found that your art supply store is your best friend. There you will usually find informed and interested sales people who are able to answer questions you didn't even know you had. They can sometimes provide manufacturer's fliers to supplement the information on product packaging. They can also recommend some of the many fine books available, and can direct you to the wide range of art classes found in many communities.

Adhesives

Paste: For very small children, paste is easier to use than glue. It is also easier for making collages that use odd materials, such as pinecones or buttons. If you use white glue these will tend to slide around and roll off before the glue sets; they will sit tight with paste.

Wheat paste: You can make your own wheat paste, which is ideal for paper mache, and for when you need large quantities.

White Glue: White glue is a mainstay of home art projects. It is available in a washable formula, and found everywhere art, craft and school supplies are sold.

Fabric Glue: This usually looks very similar to white glue, but it is formulated to withstand washing when used to glue things onto fabric. It is usually found in fabric and craft shops.

Starch: Household starch brushed onto tissue paper will make the tissue adhere to a collage, a bottle, a box...It will also stiffen fabrics and papers for three dimensional effects in collage.

Glue Guns: These electric gun-shaped appliances melt sticks of glue. With the pull of a "trigger" a drop of the hot melted glue is put into place. It dries rapidly as it cools, and is generally more successful with odd shapes and materials than white glue. Glue guns are sold in art stores and craft shops. *Because the glue is very hot, they are not appropriate for small children.* There are lower heat models intended for children. Parents should use their judgment; you know what your child can handle.

Rubber Cement: These adhesives are designed for one purpose only - to stick paper to paper. They are difficult to use and contain toxic solvents, so they are not generally recommended for small children. "One Coat" rubber cement was designed for graphic "cut and paste" work. When carefully applied in a thin coat to one side of a piece of artwork, it can be laid down and picked up again for

---

Recipe for Wheat Paste

1/3 cup regular flour
2 tablespoons sugar
1 cup water
1/4 teaspoon oil of peppermint

Mix all the ingredients except the oil. Cook over low heat until translucent. Remove from heat and stir in the oil.

repositioning. (Regular rubber cement cannot be repositioned).

Spray Mount: This is an adhesive in a spray can. Though environmentally unfriendly and more expensive than other forms of adhesive, they are perfect for certain uses, such as neatly mounting artwork or photos onto mat board for display. Some are repositionable, and some are made specifically for photos. Always use a "spray box" when using spray mounts (*see at right*).

Electric Waxer: If you are doing a lot of graphic "cut and paste" work, you may want to invest in an electric waxer. These electric tools melt wax, that when rolled over the back of artwork, leaves a uniform coat that acts as the adhesive to an art board. *Because it uses hot, melted wax, it is not appropriate for young children, and should always be kept out of their reach while being used.* To apply, roll the waxer over the back of the art you want to stick down. *Tip: wax it before you trim it to its final size.* Lay the art into place, wax side down. When the position is correct, gently rub it to apply pressure. If you do not rub it vigorously, it can still be easily lifted up for repositioning.

Dry mounting: This is a process that you will not be able to do at home because it requires special equipment. It is the neatest way to mount art and photos on cardboard or mat board, whether or not they will also be framed. It is also one way to smooth out the wrinkled paper surface of a treasured work. Dry mounting is offered by many frame shops.

Tape: There are many kinds of tape, but the most useful for children's art are masking tape and scotch tape, because they are inexpensive and easy to use.

Another useful tape is a "low tack" tape put out by 3M, similar to their "Post-it" product. Low tack means it can be stuck down and then lifted again without ruining your surface. This tape is generally found with office supplies.

On the other end of the spectrum is duct tape, found in hardware stores. Duct tape is handy when you need a tape that is powerful and durable.

How to Make a Spray Mount Box

Take a cardboard box bigger than the largest piece of artwork you have to mount. Place a stack of newspapers on the bottom. Place the artwork face down on the newspaper surface. Spray the adhesive evenly over the back of the artwork. Lift it up carefully by the edges and mount it in place. Throw away the top piece of newspaper. Now there is a fresh sheet of newspaper on top, ready for the next mounting job.

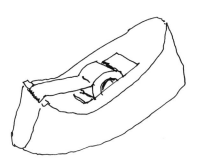

Brushes

Fine Art Brushes: These are made from either animal hair or synthetic materials. The brushes made of animal hair are more expensive, but if you take care of them, they will last much longer. With brushes you get what you pay for. Very cheap brushes will come apart as you paint in a short time.

Of the animal hair brushes, soft brushes are made from hair, stiff brushes from bristle. Watercolors usually use soft brushes, and oils and acrylics use both soft and stiff brushes.

Brushes are either round, filbert shaped, or square. The round ones are the most versatile. Brushes also come in a range of sizes, indicated by numbers. Number one is the smallest size.

Paste Brushes: These are very cheap synthetic bristle brushes that are suitable for spreading glue and paste.

House Painting Brushes: Wide paint brushes from the hardware store are useful for large color blocks. One inch and three inch brushes inspire children to try bold color strokes.

Foam Brushes: These are inexpensive brushes available at any hardware or paint supply store. They are ideal for bold brush strokes. Young children especially delight in these as a wonderful alternative to regular brushes. Also they are good for stenciling, in which the paint is dabbed onto a surface through a stencil. Because of their low cost they are an ideal alternative for materials that may damage a good brush or would be difficult to clean up.

Brush Care

Good brushes are expensive tools, so you will want your child to learn how to take proper care of them.

- Never "grind" the brush into the paint. This can break bristles. Gently dip at the paint. Remember, watercolors need a lot of water added to the paint wells in order to have enough paint to load up the brush without digging into the paint well.

- Never leave a brush bristle-side down in the paint or water container, If you are coming back after a short time, it is OK to leave a brush lying across the top of the paint or water container.

- Always wash the brush after use. Then shake it dry, and lightly smooth the bristles into shape with your fingers.

- Store brushes standing on their stick ends.

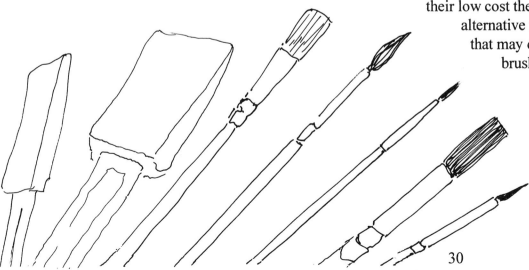

30

Clays and Modeling Compounds

Play Dough: Young children enjoy making things out of play dough. This is a good medium for the very active young child who will not normally sit down for an art project. The play dough can be hit, pounded, and squished. It can be molded over and over into different shapes. It can be dried (although it will not hold up as well as oven baked clays.) Play dough is easy to make at home (*see recipe*). Keep it in a sealed container in the refrigerator so it will remain fresh and pliable.

Modeling clays: These clays, available in a wide range of colors, are good for small children, and like play dough, they are especially good for the very active child who would rather pound something than draw. Keep it in a covered container so it will not dry out.

Air Dried Clay: These are modeling clays that get hard when exposed to air. They are usually available in white or tan (they can be painted after they dry). You can make your own - see the recipe on this page.

Warning!

Very young children are naturally tempted to try to eat clays and play dough. Keep an eye on younger siblings!

Play Dough Recipe

Mix the dry ingredients in a large sauce pan:

> 1 cup flour
> 1/2 cup salt
> 2 tablespoons Cream of Tarter

Mix the wet ingredients in a large measuring cup:

> 1 cup water
> 2 tablespoons vegetable oil
> Food coloring
> Flavor extract for scent (optional)

Add the wet ingredients to the dry and stir over medium heat until very thick. Cool and remove from pan. Store in a plastic bag so it will not dry out. Keeps almost indefinitely.

Air Dried Clay Recipe

3/4 cup regular flour
1/2 cup salt
1/2 cup cornstarch
Warm water

Add enough warm water to form a soft dough. Store in a tightly sealed plastic bag. After shaping, allow two to four days of air drying before painting.

Oven Hardening Clays: You can make your own oven-hardening clay (*see recipe this page*), or you can purchase it. The ready-made oven hardening clays are available in a broad range of colors in addition to white. The home-made clay is white, but it can be painted after firing.

After being shaped into the desired object, the clay is fired in your kitchen oven. (Be sure to follow the directions on the package if you buy your clay.) Then you can give the finished piece a topcoat of clear plastic or varnish after firing (and after painting) if you want to give it a nice gloss.

These clays are easily fashioned into little figures, creches and tableaus, boxes and bowls. They can also be used to make jewelry...beads for stringing, medallions for hanging or gluing to a pin back, shapes to glue to a barrette back. It is also fun to make little clay doll house accessories and doll "food."

Ceramic Clay: This is the traditional potters clay. You will need a kiln for firing it, because a household oven is not hot enough. *(See About Ceramic Clay, page 34.)*

Glazes: These are chemicals in liquid form that are applied to ceramic clay after the first firing, before the final firing. They are brushed on just like paint, and then in the heat of the kiln they melt to form a glassy glaze.

Plaster of Paris: This strange material comes in a powder form. Add it to water (never add water to the plaster), one cup water to one cup dry plaster. If you mix it in a cleaned milk carton, you will have a convenient pouring spout. Pour it into a mold, where it will harden. Do not EVER discard it in your drains. *In fact, keep it away from the sink at all times.* You do not want your drain pipes clogged by plaster of paris, hardened as firm as a rock. When working with plaster of paris, keep an empty container, such as an old milk carton, handy for pouring off unused portions.

Oven Hardening Clay Recipe

Mix in a large bowl:
  4 cups flour
  1 cup salt

Add to flour & salt:
  1¹/₂ cups water

Mix well, and then form into a ball. Knead the dough well for about ten minutes, and it's ready to use.

If the dough does not hold together while being worked, knead it some more.

When ready to fire, place on a baking sheet. Bake in a 250º oven for at least one hour (thick pieces may need as much as 3 hours in the oven).

You can carve plaster of paris with block carving tools *(see pages 56-57)* but as it hardens with time, the best time to do the cutting is when it has just set.

Paper Mache: Paper mache is shredded paper and paste mixed together and built up layer by layer over a base to make a lightweight shape. The base could be a balloon for a mask or piñata, a crumpled newspaper on a piece of cardboard to make a miniature hill, a wire form or cardboard tubes taped together to make a creature. When dry it can be painted. You can purchase ready-made paper mache compounds, or you can shred newspapers yourself and mix them with wheat paste *(see recipes)*.

> ## *Strip Paper Mache*
>
> **T**ear newspaper into strips. Dip each strip into a bowl of wheat paste *(see recipe, page 28)*, and pull it through two fingers to squeeze off the extra paste. The strips are then layered over your base.

Very young children find this process delightful or disgusting, depending upon their attitude about messy hands. The very young may also have trouble maintaining interest long enough to do a large paper mache project, requiring many layers before the object takes shape and before the fun of painting begins.

> ## *Pulp Paper Mache*
>
>
>
> **R**ather than building up strips of paper, this form of paper mache is handled more like modeling clay.
>
> *Tip: When you make your wheat paste for the pulp, double the amount of peppermint oil in the recipe. This helps prevent mold.*
>
> Tear the strips into one inch pieces and soak them in warm water overnight. Beat the soaked paper pieces in a kitchen mixer to make it a smooth pulp. Squeeze the pulp to strain out the water. Mix in the wheat paste until the pulp is easy to shape.

About Ceramic Clay

If you have access to a kiln for firing your clay pieces, you are truly lucky. Children love the tactile nature of clay while working with it, and they are thrilled with the finished pieces once they are fired and glazed.

To do clay projects you will need:

A good work surface. Do not cover a table with newspapers, as the newsprint will come off on the clay. A vinyl tablecloth or placemat is ideal. You may also want some burlap or an old dish towel to roll clay slabs, so they do not stick to the surface.

Clay: Kept covered in a cool place.

Slip: Clay that has been mixed with water to form a sticky paste.

Glazes

A cutting wire: You will use this to cut slabs off your block of clay as well as for trimming. Cut a piece of wire, fishing line (at least 20# test), or fine strong string, to about 18". Tie each end to a small stick. Hold a stick in each hand, and draw the wire through the clay toward you.

Clay working tools: Popsicle sticks, dull knives, forks, nails and toothpicks are all good clay tools. Use wooden dowels for rollers. Use beverage straws for punching holes.

Sponges and a container of water: These are for cleanup and to wipe any glaze that accidentally gets on the bottom of a piece. The sponges can also be used to apply slip.

When you are ready to begin:

Wedging: If your clay has not been "wedged" to eliminate air bubbles (which could cause your piece to explode during firing), you should knead it well before working with it.

Get started - refer to "Working With Clay" on page 102 for some tips.

To keep the clay workable - When you are finished for the day, but will want to keep working on the piece, cover it with a wet towel. Damp towels are also good to prevent the piece from drying too quickly and cracking. Do not allow cracks - these are weak places that can break during firing.

Firing: When your piece is complete, let it dry in a cool place. Then it needs its first firing in a kiln, called bisque firing. After this firing, the piece can be glazed and fired again.

Glazing: Apply the glaze with a brush, in thin coats. You will need to rely upon the label for the colors, as they look very different before firing! Do not apply glaze to the bottom of your piece, or it will stick to the kiln shelves. In fact, allow an unglazed 1/4" margin around the bottom edge of the piece, in case the glaze runs during firing.

Color

We are not in the habit of thinking of color as a *tool,* but in the art process it becomes a very powerful one indeed.

Colors seem to have a life of their own. They jostle and nudge each other within a multitude of varying relationships. A quiet blue may suddenly come alive when a vivid spot of orange, its complement, is placed next to it. That same blue will become almost brooding when combined with its "cool color" relative, purple. Learning to work with these relationships gives your child one more valuable art tool.

The Color Wheel: This is a color reference, a way of making the color relationships concrete and visible. Your child can fill in the color wheel shown below, or even better, make his own color wheel based upon this one.

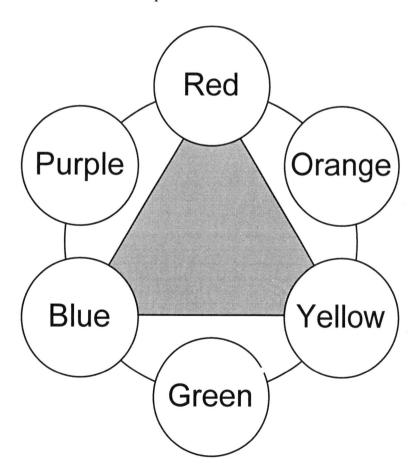

Primary Colors: These are the three basic colors - *red, blue and yellow* - from which all other colors are derived. You can see this for yourself when you mix colors. *On the color wheel shown here, the primary colors are connected by the triangle.*

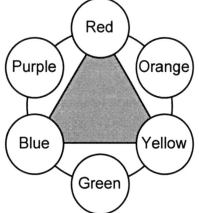

Secondary Colors: These are the three colors that are derived from the combination of two primary colors. They are Orange (from red and yellow), Green (from blue and yellow) and Purple (from red and blue).

Tertiary Colors: These are the twelve colors that are made by mixing *primary* with *secondary* colors: red-orange, orange-red, orange-yellow, yellow-orange, yellow-green, green-yellow, green-blue, blue-green, blue-purple, purple-blue, purple-red and red-purple. Because there are three colors mixed together to get the tertiaries, these colors may not be as bright as primary or secondary colors. *The Tertiary Colors are not shown on this color wheel in order to keep the wheel simple for children to color in and understand.*

Complementary Colors: When you look at the color wheel, you can see that each color has another color directly opposite it. This opposite color is the *complement* of the first color.

Complementary colors are worth exploring because they have such interesting relationships to each other:

- Complementary colors *next* to each other can add excitement to each other.
- You can deepen, darken, and gray a color by *mixing in* some of its complement.
- Shading on an object is often painted using the complement mixed in to the color of the object being painted. For example, the shading on the side of a red apple might be painted using red paint with some green mixed in.

Shades and Tints: A shade is a color mixed with black. A tint is a color that is mixed with white. Remember, when mixing tints and shades, always add the darker color to the lighter color, in small amounts at a time.

Color Mixing Rule

Always add
the darker color
to the lighter color
(never the other way
around.)

Warm and Cool Colors: If you were to draw a line straight down the middle of the color wheel from between red and purple to between green and yellow, you would find that the "cool" colors of blue, green, and purple are on one side, and the "warm" colors of red, orange and yellow are on the other. Sometimes it is interesting to do a composition that is mostly warm or mostly cool colors, and then use a color from the opposite side as an accent.

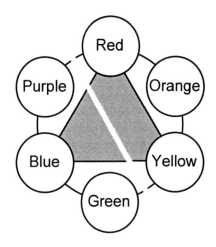

White, Black and Brown: Whether from the sun or from a light bulb, light may look "clear" or "white", but it is made up of *all* the colors. We see color when the light hits something and its pigments absorb some of the colors in the light, and reflect the rest back to our eyes (this is why we do not see colors in the dark.) When you see a blue ball, it looks blue because the ball absorbs every color except blue, and only that blue is reflected back to your eyes. You see white when *all* the colors reflect back to your eyes (imagine all those colors bouncing off the object, leaving no color on that object) and you see black when all the colors are absorbed and nothing reflects back.

So in scientific terms, white is the absence of color, and black is the saturation of color. But in real life terms, if you mixed all your paint colors together, rather than get black, you'll get something that looks more like a mucky brown!

Watch Out for the Red!

Many paint sets provide a red that is actually an *orange-red*. Because of the orange tones in the red, this is actually a tertiary color, not a primary red, and when you mix it with blue to make purple the result is a disappointing muddy brown. Fortunately, these same sets often include magenta (a deep pink red) as well. If this is the case with your paint set, use the magenta for mixing purple.

Note: It's fun to mix all the colors together to see just what you'll get. Encourage your child to do this, and other color mixing experiments, but NOT by sloshing the brush through each color in a watercolor kit. Mixed this way the paint palette will be useless until it is carefully cleaned again with a wet paper towel. Instead, try mixing the colors in a separate cup or palette.

Cutting Tools

Caution!

Some projects simply cannot be completed without a sharp cutting knife...cutting mat board, cutting foam core, trimming paper...but this is the parent's job.

No young child should be handling an Exacto knife.

Older kids, if taught how to use them, and if cautious and respectful of risky tools, may be allowed to use them.

Scissors: Get the best quality scissors that your child is able to handle. There is nothing more frustrating to a child than trying to work with scissors that will not cut properly. Small children should have scissors that are light and fit their hand, and cut paper products with ease. Older children can use adult-sized scissors. The child who has started sewing deserves a good pair of fabric scissors. These should not be used for paper projects, and their proud owner should be allowed to make them off-limits to siblings.

Exacto Knives and Utility Knives: These are knife holders with replaceable razor sharp blades. There are various sizes and shapes made for different cutting purposes. The most common Exacto size is the #11 knife and point, which looks (and cuts) like a surgeon's scalpel. Utility knives are bigger - these are good for cutting foam core board and corrugated cardboard.

Knife Blade Disposal Container: If you use cutting knives you will need a safe way to dispose of the blades. *Do not place them loose in your trash...* someone may rummage in there for a lost paper and get cut.

You can buy a container made for safe disposal, but it is easy to make one. Take an empty plastic film container, cut a slit in the lid big enough to admit a blade, and write Old Knife Blades on the top. When it is full, just toss the whole container in the trash.

Self-healing Mat: If you are doing a lot of cutting, you may want to invest in one of these mats. They are made of a plastic substance that maintains its smooth surface even when cuts are repeatedly made on it. Somehow it magically "heals" each cut. (If you do not do a lot of cutting, a piece of cardboard, especially gray chipboard, makes a perfectly fine cutting surface. Replace it when it gets too many cuts.)

Safe Cutting
with an Exacto Knife

There are several rules that you should be aware of whenever you cut with one of these sharp knives. If you follow them, you will lower your risk of an accident.

1. Use a sturdy, flat surface to make your cut. Clear away markers, notebooks, sandwiches, juice glasses, papers...

2. Place a cutting board under the item to be cut to protect your table or floor surface. Chipboard is ideal, but any form of cardboard will do.

3. Lay a metal (not plastic!) ruler down where you want to cut. (If you use plastic, you will nick it and will forever have a wavy edge.)

4. Be sure your blade is *sharp*. If it is dull you run a higher risk of hurting yourself. These blades wear out after a few uses. Make it a rule to be generous with blades. Trying to save money by getting more cuts out of one blade is a false economy...the trip to the emergency room with a bloody thumb will far outstrip the cost of new blades.

5. Hold the knife in your working hand (your right hand if you are right handed) and lay your other hand on the ruler. *Put all your weight on that ruler hand.*

6. While you have all your weight on your ruler hand, make a *light* stroke along the ruler with your blade hand. Keep the blade's sharp edge against the ruler. Do not bear down hard - this can cause your blade to skip over the material you are cutting, or worse, over the ruler and your thumb. Make several more light strokes over the first. Keep doing this until the material is cut through.

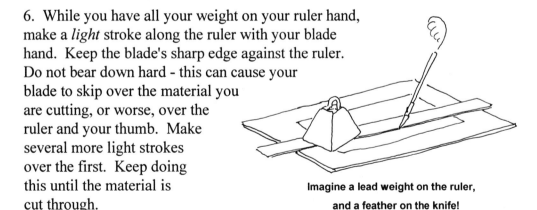

Imagine a lead weight on the ruler, and a feather on the knife!

***Remember*, keep the weight *on* the ruler hand, keep the weight *off* the blade hand, and *never* try to make the cut in one stroke.**

Drawing Mediums

Crayons: These are now available in an enormous selection of colors, including fluorescent and glitter colors.

Markers: For today's kids, markers have become even more universal than crayons. They are available with "washable" inks, recommended for smaller children. Watch out for the scented markers - these are generally indelible. Broad tips are good for larger areas of color, fine tips are good for detail. If your young child tends to use fine tipped markers a lot, with very small, highly detailed drawings, encourage the use of the large tips for a change, so your child will try a larger, looser approach. (Sometimes the fine tips can just "get lost" for awhile.)

Metallic Markers: *See Pen and Ink*

Ink: *See Pen and Ink*

Pencil: Pencils vary mostly by their softness or hardness. H pencils are hard, B pencils are soft, and HB and F pencils are in between. Within these categories there are numbers to further grade them. A soft pencil allows a dark, smudgy effect, while a hard pencil allows a light fine line. Sketching is usually done with softer pencils.

Undress Those Crayons!

As untidy as it looks, there is nothing wrong with removing the paper wraps from crayons. In fact, the paper *should* be removed so that crayons can be used on their sides. Encourage this use, especially as a technique for covering large areas in a drawing. It is also a good technique for combining colors, applying one color over another.

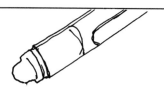

About Erasers

For young children, while any kind of soft eraser will do the job, the big pink erasers are ideal. But older children working with media such as pencil or charcoal will want to try putty erasers, available in art supply stores. These are kneaded until soft. They are gentle to the paper surface and can be shaped into a point for careful erasure of a tiny detail.

Colored Pencils: These are available in a range of colors and quality. Young children will be happy with the least expensive quality, but the older child who seriously enjoys his art should be treated to good quality colored pencils. There are also some colored pencils that are water-soluble, so that they can be worked with water to get soft blurry effects and washes.

Chalk: This is available in white and colors. It is striking on colored or black paper. For an interesting effect, dip chalk in white tempera and then apply it directly to colored construction paper. Chalk pictures need to be sprayed with fixative, if the chalk has not been used with tempera, to prevent smudging the picture after it is complete.

Charcoal: This very soft and messy material is always black. It is drawn and smudged for shading effects. The finished piece should be sprayed with fixative to prevent further - and unintended - smudging.

Conte Crayons: These short sticks of black, white, gray or brown are similar to charcoal. They are very effective on gray paper. They can be smudged for shading and highlighting effects.

Pastels: These soft chalk-like sticks are almost pure pigment. They come in a large range of colors, many of which are striking for their bold bright quality. They come in several quality grades. The best quality is "artists" quality, and is quite expensive. Start with a lower grade pastel, because it is not quite as soft as the artists quality and will be easier to handle.

Oil Pastels: These look similar to regular pastels, but they are much cheaper and considered much easier for kids to use. They do not smudge and blend as freely as pastels, but they come in the same bold bright colors. Like chalk, these are striking on colored or black paper.

Aquarelles: These look like oil pastels but they can be worked with water to get soft washes and blurred lines, with a watercolor effect. The water can be applied after the drawing has been made, or the aquarelle stick can be dipped in water before applying to the paper. Aquarelles also make excellent face paint.

> *About Fixative*
>
> **F**ixative is a spray that you apply to a finished piece. It coats the drawing so that the dust particles of the medium will no longer smudge. It is usually used with pastels, chalk and charcoal.

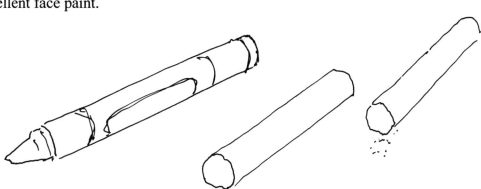

To hold your
shirt or bag flat, and
to prevent color
seeping through to the
other side, insert a
piece of cardboard
inside it, big enough
to stretch it flat.
Cover the cardboard
first with plastic wrap,
taping it into place.

Fabric Decoration

Squeeze-Tube Dimensional Paints: These are paints available in a wide range of colors, including opalescent and glitter colors, that come in small plastic squeeze tube containers with pointed tips. They are squeezed directly onto the fabric where they take the three-dimensional shape of a squirt of toothpaste, only smaller.

Very young children will have fun just making squiggles in various colors, while older children will enjoy using these paints for writing on fabric, and to make formal designs incorporating other materials, such as buttons, bows, sequins and rosettes.

After the finished design has been allowed to dry (it can take days) they can go through the washer and dryer on lower heat settings. Until they dry, they are water soluble for easy cleanup. These paints are generally found in craft and fabric shops.

These paints are ideal for small children, and fun for birthday party projects, where everyone brings something to decorate (a hat, a T-shirt, a pair of tennis shoes) and the host provides the squeeze paints.

Tie Dye

To tie dye, simply bunch up your clean cotton cloth and tie rubber bands around the bunches. You can twist the bunches for a nice effect.

Dip the cloth into a prepared fabric dye. You can undo some of the bunches when dipping into a second color. *(See Color, page 35, for help mixing colors.)* Rinse well, *twice,* in cold water, between colors and when finished, and hang it up to dry. Be sure the fabric is completely dry before removing the rubber bands.

Fabric Crayons: These are special crayons made to draw on paper first; then the picture is transferred by ironing onto the fabric (follow the directions on the packaging). They are easier for small children to use than paints, but you will want to be sure these very pricey crayons do not get mixed up with their humble, and inexpensive, lookalikes.

Fabric Paint: These opaque paints look like tempera, but remain flexible after being painted on fabric. After being set with heat, they can be machine washed. Most can be set simply with a hot household iron. Fabric paints are available in a wide range of colors, including opalescent.

Silk Paints and Dyes: These dye colors, unlike fabric paints, are made for working on silk. They are used with a resist (called gutta, pronounced "goo-tah) and then painted or applied with a tiny dropper, within the resist lines (which keep the colors from running into each other). You can also paint without resist, with a watercolor effect, allowing colors to blend together.

True dyes are more difficult to work with, so start out with silk *paints*. They are available in water soluble formulas for easy cleanup, and are set with a household iron.

Jewelry Making

The range of jewelry making activities is enormous. Included here are some of the things you may need for some of the simpler activities, such as bead stringing. There are all kinds of creative things that children can do with beads, including making their own beads with oven-baked clays. (*For jewelry-making ideas, see pages 103 and 131-132.*)

Except where otherwise noted, these materials are generally available in craft shops, bead shops, and sometimes in fabric shops.

Needle Nose Pliers: These indispensable pliers have small pointed tips, absolutely necessary for opening and closing tiny jewelry clasps and rings. They can be found in hardware stores as well as craft shops.

Beading Board: If you do a lot of bead stringing, a beading board can make it easier to line the beads up so they don't roll about with a life of their own. Beading boards are usually rather inexpensive, made of flocked styrene with wells for holding beads and grooves for lining up beads without spills.

Findings: This is a general name for the rings, clasps and connectors used in making earrings, necklaces and bracelets. These include clasps, earring wires, ear studs, wires for stringing beads for earrings, jump rings and cord crimps. You can also get barrette clasps and pin clasps.

Leather Thong and Silk Cord: These are thick laces for stringing beads. You need to use beads with large holes to accommodate the size of the cord. When complete the ends can be tied in a knot (but make sure the necklace will fit over a head without untying) or finished with a clasp.

Stringing Thread: Silk, nylon or cotton thread are all available for stringing beads. Choose a color that is closest to the predominant color of the beads you are stringing.

Nylon Thread, Thin Fishing Line: Bead shops sell a nylon thread that is similar to thin fishing line. Both are very strong and can be used for stringing beads, but knots may come undone unless pulled very tight.

Tigertail: This is a very strong plastic-coated wire, ideal for stringing heavy beads.

Elastic Thread: This is an easy alternative for small children. They can string beads on the elastic, and finish it off by tying the ends into a knot. It will stretch to fit over the head.

Beads: Bead shops and craft shops have all kinds of beads available to spark the imagination. There are bright plastic and painted wooden beads, natural colored wooden and clay beads, bright ceramics, glass beads, crystal beads, horn, amber, jade, onyx, and semi-precious stone beads, and many many more.

Better yet, kids can make their *own* beads out of clay, and then paint them. They can even make beads out of brightly colored magazine pages (*see page 132*).

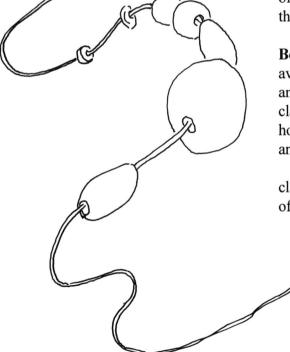

Necklace Making for Young Hands

Small children will find clasps and pliers difficult to operate. They are more successful when they string beads on thick thongs or elastic, and then tie the ends in a knot. You will need to help them with the knotting at first, to show them how to make the necklace long enough to slip over a head without needing a clasp!

To Finish with an End Clasp

On a thick thong or cord: Place the lace end in the open end of a lace end crimp (A). Close the sides of the crimp down on the lace, using needle nose pliers (B). Attach a clasp to the ring at the end of the crimp (C).

On thread, thin fishing line or Tigertail: When you are finished stringing the beads, tie a knot in the end of the thread, as close to the last bead as possible (A). Hold the end knot in place on an end crimp (B), put a dab of white glue on the knot (fabric glue is best), and tighten the crimp over the knot with the pliers. It closes on its hinge over the knot (C). *Note: Some crimps need to be put into place as the first bead to be strung.*

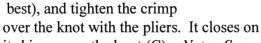

Opening a Jump Ring

Jump rings are the tiny gold or silver circles used to connect parts of a piece of jewelry. Do not open a jump ring by pulling it apart into an oval. This will weaken it. Instead, pull the two ends *sideways* away from each other. Then pinch them back into the original circle shape.

NO   YES

Nature's Materials

Dried Leaves, Flowers, Grasses: Hang them upside-down to dry in a dry place, out of direct sunlight. Or press them in paper towels under stacks of books. Use them to make rubbings, use them as weaving materials in weavings and hangings, and use them in collages.

Driftwood: Use in wooden construction and sculptures, hangings and collages.

Nutshells: Use in collages. In miniature worlds you can use walnut shell halves for tiny boats or beds, smaller nutshells for food and drinking vessels.

Pinecones: Use in collages. Use to make ornaments, glued to Styrofoam spheres. Use to decorate picture frames.

Sea Shells: Use in collages, or to decorate picture frames and treasure boxes. Use shells with holes in them to string up on mobiles or hangings.

Seedpods: Use in collages.

Twigs: Willow, honeysuckle, wisteria and grapevine twigs are all flexible enough to construct little "log" houses or furniture, and the honeysuckle and wisteria are especially easy for young children to weave into hangings and wreaths.

For projects using these natural materials, see collages, weaving, environments (page 105), treasure boxes (page 114), and gifts (pages 131-135).

Paints

Paints come in a wide range of materials, some water soluble, some oil based. Some paints that are not specifically formulated for young children do contain toxic materials, so you should read the labels, especially if you have very small children. Another concern you may have when working with young children is whether the paints are washable.

Tempera: This is a low cost, non-toxic, opaque paint, available in pre-mixed or powder forms, with a wide range of colors, including florescent and opalescent. The opalescent gold and silver really *look* metallic, and children love them. Tempera is also available in "washable" formulas, making these ideal for young children. (Adding some dish washing detergent to the paint is another way to make it more washable.)

Finger paints: These thick paints delight young children who can't resist its tactile quality. You can make your own finger paints with the recipe shown here. Butcher paper is good for finger-painting because it has a glossy side that does not absorb the paint.

About Painting Tools

The imagination is the limit when it comes to painting tools. Paint brushes are just a start. Paint can be applied with all kinds of fascinating effects with fingers, palms, sponges, crumpled paper, pot scrubbers, combs, spatulas, Q-tips. Dip string in the paint and lay it on paper. Try blowing the paint on the paper with a straw. Cross into the realm of printing with corks, potato stamps, thumb prints. (A trout makes a terrific fish imprint - what a way to immortalize that first catch! - and if you use non-toxic paints, can be cleaned off in time to prepare it for dinner.)

These sessions can get quite lively as the imagination starts soaring, so you might want to get it started in an invulnerable place...outside, or in the garage or basement. Do protect the family cat from paw print experiments, though, as she will want to lick her feet off afterward, and the paint could make her sick.

Recipe for Finger Paint

1 part cornstarch mixed with cold water to make a paste
3 parts boiling water
Powdered tempera

In a saucepan mix the cornstarch with the cold water to make a paste. When it is smooth, add the boiling water, stirring constantly. Cook on medium heat until the mixture is translucent. Add tempera until the color reaches the intensity that appeals to you.

About Using Watercolors

The more serious artist will need:

Watercolors - tubes or blocks

Watercolor brushes (soft brushes) - at *least three brushes:* one large one for washes, one medium round brush, and one small pointed brush for detail.

Drawing board (ready-made, chipboard or plywood) - to support the paper. Use clips, rubber bands or masking tape to attach your paper to the board.

Watercolor paper - Thinner papers should be stretched to keep from wrinkling.

      To stretch watercolor paper: *Place one piece of paper on your drawing board. Wet the paper with a damp sponge. Gently smooth the paper flat with a clean cloth, working from the center and out to the edges. Tape the edges down to the board with masking tape or gummed mailing tape. Allow the paper to dry before using it.*

Palette - You will need a mixing surface. Ideally you will want lots of little wells in the palette (or many little pots) so colors will not run together.

Frisket *(optional)* - A protective cover applied to the paper to keep it free of paint where you want the paper to stay clean. A frisket can be painted over, and later removed, revealing the clean area underneath in the shape of the frisket. 3M's low tack tape works well. Or, rubber cement can be brushed on thickly to act as a frisket, and later rubbed off when completely dry.

Drawing pencil (HB or B) for light preliminary sketch

Water, rags and sponges

Watercolors: These are transparent paints mixed with water. They are available very reasonably priced in dime stores as boxed palettes with one or two rows of color wells, and with mixing wells on the inside of the lid. They are also available as student quality and artist quality paints in tubes or blocks. (*Note: paints in tubes are easier to mix, but they may tend to harden with time.*)

Low cost water-color sets are excellent for young children, although the brushes included in these sets are generally very poor quality. You will want to supplement the set with two watercolor brushes, one medium, one large. Older children will want a small brush as well. Young children will be happy using watercolors on just about any heavy paper.

As your child matures and develops her skills with watercolors, she deserves to work with finer materials, and will appreciate the student or artist grade of watercolors and real water-color papers. She also deserves to learn to use them correctly. Libraries, book shops and art supply stores have good books providing useful technical information. An older student may want to take an adult watercolor class, offered in many communities.

Guache: These paints are similar to watercolors, but they have a white pigment added to make them opaque. Guache is not as dependent upon the quality of the paper as are watercolors.

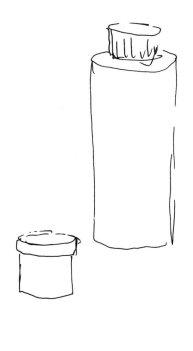

Acrylics: These are fast drying, bright colored paints. Some acrylics can be used on a variety of surfaces, including wood, plaster, metal or glass, making them ideal for many craft purposes. They are also commonly used in airbrushes. Acrylics are easier than oils for children to handle, as they are water soluble, but some acrylics dry so rapidly that they are difficult to rework. They have a wide range of textures, however, depending upon the "medium" that can be mixed in. Most common are mediums to produce matte or gloss effects, but there are also mediums to make interesting textures, such as coarse or fine sand, the appearance of fibers, or the look of stucco. Acrylics are available in jars (for thinner paint) or tubes (for thicker paint, similar to oils).

Oils: Oil paints contain pigment bound with oil for a translucent effect. They are sold in tubes, in two grades, student grade and artists grade. The artist grade is better quality, with stronger colors more resistant to fading. It is also more expensive. Very messy, and slow to dry, it is better to keep oils off limits for younger children. Teens will nonetheless find its slow-drying quality a boon, because it allows time to make corrections. All kinds of effects are possible with oils, from transparent washes to thick palette knife application.

Primer: White primer is a handy paint to keep on hand. It is available in most hardware stores and any paint store. It is made to cover just about any material, producing a good paintable surface. Use it to paint cookie tins so your child can decorate them to be canisters. Use it to paint an old piece of furniture so your teen can paint it imaginatively for his room. Use it to prepare hardboard to be a canvas for oils or acrylics.

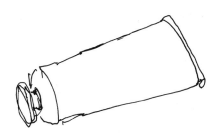

About using Oils

You will need:

Oil paints, starting with about 10 or 11 colors (mix for more).
Brushes - at least three, one small soft pointed brush, and two larger stiff brushes.
Palette - a flat board, tin lid or an old plate will do. You do not want a surface that will absorb the paint. It should be plain colored.
Palette knife - a flexible flat tool for mixing paint.
Medium cups, one for linseed oil and one for turpentine. There are sets that clip to the palette.
Painting surface - stretched canvas or prepared hardboard. *To prepare your own hardboard, sand it first with fine sandpaper, and then paint it with white primer.*
Cleaning materials - Paint thinner, rags, a bar of soap
Easel - optional but not necessary. Your canvas can be leaned on a chair or propped on a table.

To start your painting:

Oil painting can be very messy, so be sure to protect the floor and your clothing.

Start out with a light sketch in pale brown or blue, using a small pointed brush. Squeeze the paint out a little bit at a time onto the palette. Using the palette knife, mix the paint with some turpentine, a few drops at a time, to make it thinner. *Always use the palette knife for mixing*, so that your expensive brushes will not be ruined.

It is a good idea to start out with thinned paints in the beginning of the painting, using only turpentine mixed with the paint. Then build up the picture surface with thicker, richer paints using linseed oil in addition to the turpentine.

If you make a mistake, scrape the paint off with the palette knife, rub the area with a rag dipped in paint thinner or turpentine, and then rework it.

When complete, allow the painting to dry in a dust-free area. It may even take months for a painting to dry. Meanwhile, proper cleanup is essential. *Never* allow paint to harden on brushes or on the palette, as this will ruin them. Wipe brushes with a rag, and then rinse them in paint thinner. Next wash them well with soap and water. Dry them, smooth them into shape, and store them lying down or standing on their wooden ends. Be sure all caps are tightly screwed onto paint tubes.

Palettes

Small Round Plastic Palettes: These are usually about 7" in diameter, and have 10 to 12 small wells to hold paints in a circle. The large well in the center can be used for mixing colors. These are excellent for young children who will not be doing a lot of color mixing (there is not much room for mixing on these palettes) and who will not need large amounts of paint.

"Muffin Tin" Palettes: These hold much more paint in each well, but do not have a mixing area. They are good for small children who will not be doing much mixing, and will need large amounts of paint (typically tempera).

Multi-well Palettes: These tend to be larger, with a lot of room for mixing paints. These are suitable for all ages and a variety of paint types.

Storage Palettes: These are palettes with covers so that leftover paint and mixed colors remain workable. Fast drying acrylics are easier to work with in these covered palettes, as the cover will slow their drying time during use.

Recycled Palettes: Small containers with lids, such as babyfood jars or lunch box sized cottage cheese containers, make excellent paint containers. Additional small containers can be used to mix colors.

Oil Palette: A piece of Formica or clean hardboard will make a good palette for oil painting. A white background makes it easier to mix colors.

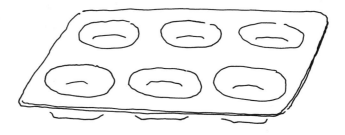

Papers

Papers come in many sizes and weights, in pads or in single sheets, and with various textures. Smooth papers are good for detailed work, such as pencil or pen and ink. Rough textured papers are ideal for media that allow the texture to show through, such as charcoal or pastels.

Their weight, shown as pounds, refers to their thickness, and this can range from very light translucent paper to something as thick as cardboard. Some better quality papers are made of cotton rag, and their "rag content" is shown on the package as a percentage.

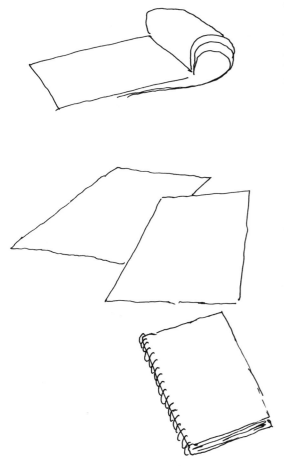

Construction Paper: This paper is available in a range of qualities, in many colors. Use for drawing (especially with chalk or pastels) and collages.

Newsprint: This is an inexpensive, smooth, very lightweight paper with a grayish color.

Manila Drawing Paper: This inexpensive, smooth, creamy colored paper is available in several weights.

White Drawing Paper: This is available in light (50#) to heavy weight (90#) papers, that are generally smooth, and moderately priced.

Charcoal Paper: This has a rougher texture (and is generally more expensive) than white drawing papers. It is available in a range of weights.

Watercolor Paper: This is a very heavy bodied paper with a distinctively textured surface. Generally, the higher the rag content the higher the quality (and the cost). Its weight also affects the price. Less expensive student grades are usually about 90# to 130#. This is not as hefty as some of the professional quality papers that range up to around 300#.

Printing Paper: This is a fine, cloth-like paper, usually rice paper, made to take a clear impression.

Tracing paper: These translucent papers range from very inexpensive lightweight pads or rolls, to very heavy parchments.

Metallic Paper: These are foil-like papers that can be used in bookmaking, decorating boxes, collage or mounting artwork.

Tissue Paper: Tissue papers are lightweight, translucent papers available in a wide range of colors. You can buy them in packages by color or in assorted packs. These can be used in collages with common household starch as a gluing medium.

Origami Papers: These packages of square paper, often covered with lovely patterns, are meant for origami, the Japanese paper folding craft, but they are very special for decorating boxes, making collages...

Handmade Papers: There are beautiful handmade papers with all sorts of interesting colors and flecks of material in them. These are purchased by the sheet. They can be used in making beautiful books, for printing, for decorating boxes, for framing, for very sophisticated collage work...

Recycled Papers: Younger children are quite happy drawing on the blank side of discarded photocopies, report pages and forms. Discarded letterhead, from firms that are relocating or changing names, provide good quality paper stock with interesting textures; just cut off the edge of the page where the firm name is printed. Paper scraps are good for collages.

The Quality of the Paper

It is believed by some that the paper your very young child uses should all be of the highest quality, to encourage and honor the child's artwork. Others believe that for the very young, the quality of the paper is far less important than the quantity of it, and give their children reams of "recycled" paper that may be printed on one side.

In defense of recycling, it is morally on the side of the angels, and far less expensive than buying good - and costly - paper. It is disconcerting to see a small child make a scribble in the middle of a clean sheet of paper and then move on to the next one. A good compromise...if you can get your hands on discarded office letterhead, you can get very nice quality paper.

And good materials *are* inspiring. In fact, if you choose to use mostly recycled papers, *do* treat your child to good quality paper now and then.

Finally, you have to realize that Murphy's Law applies to art just like everything else. If you provide recycled paper, the day will inevitably come when your child will do a stunning painting on the back of a school notice, you will want to frame it, and the printing on the other side will show through. One parent will be appalled, another may find this part of its charm. You'll have to work this out for yourself.

Railroad Board, Poster Board, Tag board: Low cost and available in colors, these range from very stiff paper to cardboard weights.

Bristol: This is a very lightweight cardboard with a smooth drawing surface.

Illustration Board: This is cardboard with a fine drawing surface. The higher the rag content the higher the quality.

Scratch Board: This is a board with a black surface overlaid on a white one. A special scratch knife is used to scratch lines through the black surface, revealing the white clay surface beneath, with a dramatic white on black drawing effect. Some are foil underneath instead of white, and some are textured.

Newsboard, Chipboard: This is a very stiff, sturdy, and inexpensive gray cardboard, good for mounting and for collages.

Corrugated Board: Everyone is familiar with this cardboard, which is commonly used for shipping cartons. While generally brown, it is sometimes available in art stores with a white paper surface on one side. This is a very sturdy, lightweight and inexpensive alternative for mounting and for collages.

Foam Core: This is an extremely lightweight, sturdy board generally available in 1/8" to 1/2" thicknesses. Foam Core is actually Styrofoam sandwiched between two sheets of exceptionally smooth white paper, with a good surface for ink and paints. It is used for display, for dry mounting artwork, and as a high quality base board for collage.

Architects use it for building models, by cutting pieces and gluing them together. If an adult cuts the pieces (it should be done with a very sharp cutter, such as an Exacto knife) a child could have a wonderful time assembling pieces into a sculpture or a building model of her own *(see Constructions page 97.)*

Pen and Ink

Pen and ink is used for both drawing and calligraphy. There are kits that teach calligraphy, many including pens, ink, a ruled practice pad, fine parchment, and instructions.

Pen Holders: These are pen handles with a place at one end to accept a pen tip. This allows for economy and flexibility, as many different types of tips can be inserted and used for various effects.

Pen Tips: These are the metal tips that fit into pen holders. They range from very fine points for extremely thin lines, to flat points for lettering.

Technical Pens: These pens are precision instruments that make an exceptionally smooth, uniform line. (They are sometimes called capillary pens because the ink is drawn from the ink well to the tip by capillary action.) The sketches in this book were drawn with a technical pen. These pens are available with a broad range of tip sizes, and some are available with convenient cartridge ink refills. It is very important that these fine (and expensive) pens be kept clean. They are not for careless artists or for the young.

India Ink: This is an opaque black ink, made from carbon pigment. A high quality india ink will not fade or gray.

Technical Ink: This is an ink that has been formulated so that it will not clog technical pens.

Colored Ink: These are fun because they produce brilliant colors. They are sometimes called watercolor inks, and can be handled just like watercolors. As they are not washable, they may not be appropriate for some young children.

Sharpie Pens: These are markers that will write on virtually any surface. They are available with office supplies as well as art supplies. Sharpies are indelible - you may wish to keep them out of the hands of very young children. They are available in black and a few other colors, and in extra fine, fine, medium or thick points. The thick point makes a wonderful fat line.

Metallic Markers: These are markers that have a metallic substance suspended in the ink so that they actually look like gold leaf or silver foil. They are relatively expensive, messy and bothersome to use (they must be nursed along to maintain a smooth flow) and they are also indelible. This can translate to a big mess in the hands of small children.

All this aside, metallic markers are thrilling to use. They can approximate the look of medieval illumination, especially when used with calligraphy. Some are available with chisel tips for lettering. They can add beautiful accents to colored pencil or pastel drawings, and they are lovely on greeting cards.

Printing Materials

Household Stamps: Every household has materials that make good printing stamps. Children enjoy experimenting with sponges, forks, corks, building blocks, and other interesting shapes dipped into paint and stamped on paper.

Potato Stamp: This is the easiest of the cut block printing methods. Cut a potato in half. Carve a shape on it and cut away all the background. Dip it into paint or on a stamp pad and stamp it on the paper.

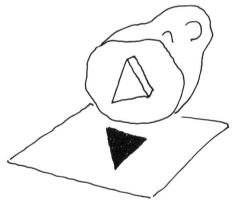

Plaster Stamp: You can make your own plaster stamps by mixing plaster of paris (*see page 32*) and pouring it in a paper cup. As soon as it hardens, remove it from the cup, and carve your stamp shape on one end with block cutters.

Wood Linoleum Blocks: These are wooden blocks with linoleum laminated to one side. They are available in many sizes. An image is cut into the linoleum with a sharp carving tool.

Some linoleum blocks are harder to carve than others. The harder the linoleum is to cut, the more likely the knife will slip and hurt the cutter, so try to get the softer grades of linoleum for children. In addition, this material can get brittle as it ages. If the block your child is trying to cut is hard and brittle, it may have been on a shop shelf too long. Do not continue to use it, as your child's hands will surely get cut in the process.

Unmounted Linoleum: These are less expensive than wood linoleum blocks. They are simply pieces of linoleum backed with jute.

Rubber-like Blocks: These can be a safe alternative for younger children, as they can be cut without exerting much force. Some are available as "make your own stamp" kits.

Block Cutters: These are special cutting tools for print blocks, with a sharp cutting edge set on a handle. They are made to gouge the block surface and scoop it away. There is a block cutter shown on the cover of this book, next to the blue tube of paint.

Brayers: These are rollers with handles for applying printing ink smoothly and uniformly.

Printing Inks: These are available in both water-soluble and oil-based formulations.

Transferring a Drawing

You will usually want to work up a drawing on scratch paper, and then transfer it to the block surface. (Use this method any time you want to transfer an image to a new surface.)

To transfer your image:

1. Turn the drawing over. With a soft pencil, rub back and forth on the back of the drawing, leaving a gray area of graphite. You do not have to cover the parts of the drawing that are blank, but you must cover the backs of all your drawing's lines.

Drawing on front side   *Pencil on reverse*

2. Place the drawing, right side up, on the block (or paper) that you are transferring to. Make sure that it is lined up just the way you want it.
3. Firmly draw over your drawing. The graphite on the reverse will transfer the lines lightly to the new surface.

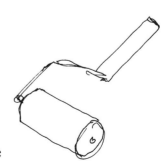

About Block Printing

In its simple forms, experimenting with printing is a lot of fun for all ages. Young children love printing with potato stamps and household objects. Older kids and teens enjoy linoleum blocks. The teen who would like to explore other more sophisticated forms of printing should seek out classes to learn the techniques in a hands-on setting.

How to block print:

1. Prepare a design. Work it up on paper first, continually reworking it to simplify the lines.

2. Transfer the design to the surface of the block (*See page 57*).

3. Cut out the design, cutting away the "negative" space with a block cutter. *The negative space is the part of the design that will not have ink - it will be the color of the paper.* Set the block on a folded towel to keep it from skidding, and cut with slow controlled pressure, not allowing the knife to skip or gouge too deeply. Always cut *away* from yourself.

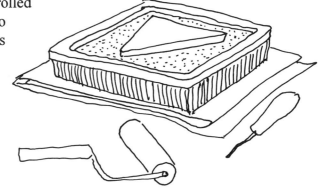

4. Squeeze some ink onto a piece of glass or Plexiglas. Roll the brayer back and forth until the ink is a fine film. Pass the roller back and forth on the block until it has been uniformly inked.

5. Carefully lay a piece of paper on the block. *Don't move it or the image will blur.* Lay a piece of heavy paper or light card stock over the paper and rub it with a large spoon. Lift the print off.

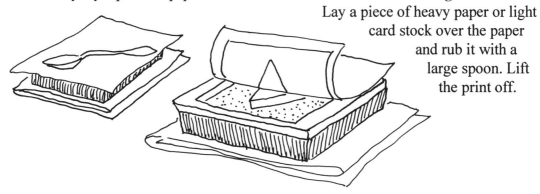

About Stenciling

Stenciling is not exactly printing, but has many similarities. When you make a stencil, you can make multiples of one image, just as you can with printing.

Coloring with their own original stencils, using crayons, pastels, markers or colored pencils, children can create beautifully patterned artwork. With their stencils and fabric paints, children can decorate T-shirts, pillows, hats and tote bags. With household paint their stencils can be used to decorate boxes, playhouse walls, and canisters. With acrylics or temperas they can stencil greeting cards.

To make a stencil:

1. Prepare your design. Draw it on paper and simplify it as much as possible.

2. Trace it onto cardboard or heavy paper (*see Transferring a Drawing, page 57*). If using cardboard, an adult may need to cut out the stencil (an Exacto knife will make the most precise cut). For younger children, see the tip on page 87.

3. Hold the stencil firmly in place on the paper and apply the medium. Rub crayons, pencils, markers or pastels back and forth over the opening. Apply paint and fabric paint with a brush or sponge (sponge brushes are ideal), dabbing the visible paper or fabric, taking care the paint does not get under the stencil.

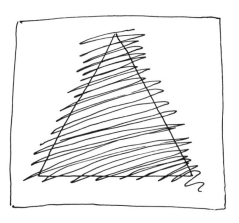

Protective Finishes

Sometimes we want to give a piece of artwork a protective coating. Sometimes we just want a glossier surface. There are all kinds of clear finishes that you can apply to your work. Look in paint and hardware stores as well as art or craft supply stores.

Brush-On Finishes: For most children, this is the easiest form to work with. There are all kinds, from polyurethane and acrylic finishes to clear gloss enamel and old fashioned shellac. Read labels carefully to make sure this is a product that you want your child to handle. If it is, transfer a small amount into a small container (such as a margarine tub or yogurt cup) so that spills and accidents can be kept to a minimum. Work over a stack of newspapers, and throw away the top sheet when it gets too many drips on it.

Spray Finishes: This is less environmentally friendly, and more difficult for children than the brush-on finishes, but adults favor the spray method because it is usually faster and covers evenly. To keep the mess to a minimum, spray the item while it is in a cardboard box, similar to a spray mount box *(see page 29)*. Be sure to work with good ventilation, and read the directions on the spray can.

Decoupage Glue: This is a white glue that dries clear and has a glossy plastic finish. It is good for jewelry and small collages. It is usually only to be found in craft stores.

Acrylic Sheets: If you want to have the protection of a piece of glass without its weight, you could put a sheet of acrylic over a flat piece of art. These are available in various weights, and can be found in graphic design and architect's supply stores.

Lamination: There are special machines that will encase a flat object (such as a drawing) in plastic. This is a service that is available in some photocopy shops (check your yellow pages for other sources). This is a great way to protect a book cover, and to make place mats and coasters *(see page 133)*.

Clear Contact Paper: If lamination is too expensive or not available, clear contact paper can be used for a similar effect. But this is not a project for the younger children. They will be frustrated by the material, which has a tendency to turn over and stick on itself, flop down crookedly, or get enormous bubbles encased in the middle. Be sure to rub it down *as you lay it down* to work out air bubbles. Better yet, practice on something else to get the hang of it before you tackle a prized work of art.

Recycled Materials

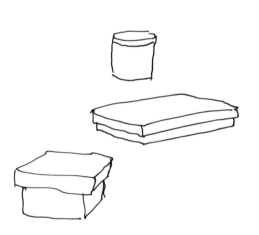

Beverage Straws: Cut these up and string them as a necklace. Use to blow paint for an interesting effect. Use to poke neat holes in clay.

Boxes: Good sturdy boxes are always worth saving. Very large boxes, such as appliance cartons, can be made into puppet theaters, caves, club houses and play houses. Large boxes can be made into vehicles and doll houses *(page 105)*. Small boxes can become buildings in a "miniature world" *(page 97)*. Unusual, interesting boxes can be decorated to hold treasures *(page 114)*.

Buttons: String to make necklaces, sew as a fanciful trim to tennis shoes and T-shirts, use in collages.

Circuit Wire: Use in collage, use in weavings and hangings, and to make wire sculpture and wire figures.

Construction Scraps: Pieces of wood are good for wooden constructions (with smaller children, be sure the wood is soft enough to *easily* hammer a nail into it.) Wire, PVC pipe, copper tubing...these are all good in mobiles, wooden constructions, and collages.

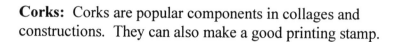

Corks: Corks are popular components in collages and constructions. They can also make a good printing stamp.

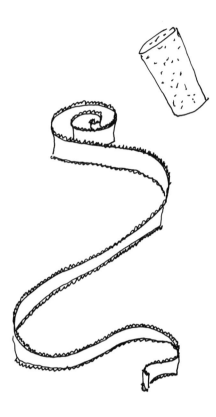

Fabric and Trim Scraps: Use in collages, use to make doll clothes and blankets, use in rag rugs. Velvets make good dollhouse rugs. Shoulder pads can be sewn together to make a doll pillow, or with one side open, a purse.

Film Containers: These are useful in collages, in constructions, and to hold small treasures for jewelry making or collage.

Gift Wrap and Ribbon: Even the discards after unwrapping gifts can be used in collages and to cover boxes. Gift wrap is also a less expensive alternative to Origami paper.

Greeting Cards: Cut these apart and use as elements in collages.

Kitchen Stuff: Macaroni, rice, seeds, dried corn, dried beans...all of these are wonderful in collages. Beans can be glued onto a Styrofoam ball to make an ornament *(page 133)* and glued onto a picture mat to make a frame *(page 134)*. And don't forget potatoes, the natural printing stamp.

Lids: Metal frozen juice concentrate lids, bottle caps and plastic juice lids are easily nailed onto wood constructions, and can be used in collages. Concentrate lids make perfect bases for making jewelry pins and magnets *(page 132-133)*.

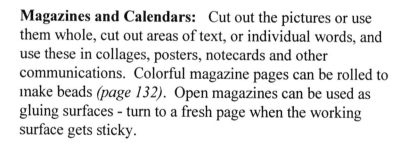

Magazines and Calendars: Cut out the pictures or use them whole, cut out areas of text, or individual words, and use these in collages, posters, notecards and other communications. Colorful magazine pages can be rolled to make beads *(page 132)*. Open magazines can be used as gluing surfaces - turn to a fresh page when the working surface gets sticky.

Mat Board Cutouts: Frame shops usually discard the center pieces they cut out of mat board. These are terrific for making collages because they are strong enough to support heavy materials and are usually an attractive color and texture.

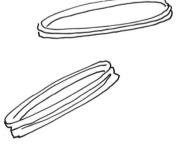

Office Supplies: Discarded letterhead makes great drawing paper. Forms and other papers that are blank on one side are fine for drawing on the reverse. (Also, forms and envelopes are great fun when playing "business").

Packing Materials: Styrofoam packing shapes are perfect for constructions. They can also be used for printing blocks. Plastic bubble wrap can also be used for printing. Use packing "popcorn" in collages, or to string together for necklaces or Christmas tree decorations.

Paper Bags: They are perfect for puppets (the white bags are especially nice because they take color very well).

Photos: Extra or unwanted prints can take on new life cut up in collages with family, activity or holiday themes.

Spools: Use in constructions, or paint and thread on a cord to be a necklace.

String: Use in collages, use in mobiles.

Tiles: Small tiles are good in collages. Large tiles are useful in constructions. Groups of tiles make an interesting surface for making prints.

Wallpaper Sample Books: When new wallpaper lines come out, dealers throw away the outdated sample books. These are gold mines of beautiful paper for making collages, decorating boxes *(page 114)*, book covers *(page 119)*, making greeting cards *(page 125)* and paper jewelry *(page 132)...*

Yarn: Use for texture in collages, for weaving, as hair on puppets and clothes-pin dolls *(pages 108-109)*.

Unclassified Stuff

     Some materials defy classification. They just don't fit into any of the other groupings So here they are, lumped together whether they like it or not.

Clear Plastic - Available by the yard in fabric stores, this plastic can be sewn. This is fun to use to make "souvenir" pouches and bookmarks. There are also sheets of clear acrylic available from graphic and architect supply stores.

Vinyl Type: These are letters and numbers made of vinyl, that can give the look of typeset printing. They are available in colors, black, white, gold and silver, usually packaged by size and color, and found in stationery and art supply stores.   These letters are useful to label containers, for book titles, posters, and collage.

     To use them, just lift a letter from the sheet with a fingernail, tweezers, or the tip of an exacto knife blade, and carefully lay it in place without pressing on it. Place the remaining letters of the word the same way.   Lift each letter again and again to reposition it until all the letters are straight and in just the right position. Then press down on them, to adhere them to the surface.

     You can also use them as a mask (a reverse stencil). Lay the letters down but do not press them too firmly to the surface. Paint over them, and then pull each letter up...the paper color shape of the letter will remain in the painted area.

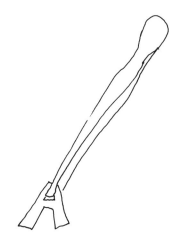

Section Three

So Much To Do!

Projects & Ideas

Every child is an artist.
The problem is how to remain
an artist once he grows up.

Pablo Picasso

So Much to Do!
Projects & Ideas

Sometimes your resident artist will need an idea to set him off and running in a new creative direction. Grouped by category, the project ideas described in this section are just that - *ideas*. They are not detailed blueprints for specific results. They are meant to be starting points, inspirations. You can suggest them just as they are to your child, or modify them in any way you like. While some projects here have specific step-by-step directions to teach a process or technique, most are quite open ended.

They can be used in different ways for different age groups and abilities. In fact, the difference between a young child and a teen is usually in the way they *solve* a project problem, not the *project* itself. Sometimes the young child will not understand the concept behind a project - stenciling, for example - but being exposed to it may lead to something new, and in the future, stenciling will make more sense. Meanwhile, if he cuts out a stencil and glues the shape onto paper instead of stenciling with it, then the project has simply moved to collage...no harm done!

Finally, parents should be aware that some of these projects are so much fun that everyone wants to get in the act. Even if you never considered yourself an artist, you may find yourself doing more and more art as your child opens these doors of opportunity with you.

Enjoy!

Painting and Drawing

For a White Border:

Put a border of low tack tape *(see page 29)* around the edge of the paper before starting to paint. This will create a white border when it is removed. For some reason this looks terrific!

There is more to drawing and painting than just sitting down to a white sheet of paper with crayons or paint. Simple suggestions can broaden or change your child's focus, even send her in a new direction. In this section you will find some ideas for...a new *subject* to draw...a new *material* to stimulate discovery...a new *technique* to get the creative wheels turning. (***Note:*** You will notice that as they go along, some of the ideas become more appropriate for older children.)

You'll see that a lot of these encourage abstract work. It is in doing abstract work that we become most aware of color, texture, composition. Another reason to encourage abstract work is to free us all from the conventional wisdom that good draftsmanship is the only path to good art.

Kids who are interested in becoming good "drawers" will usually become that through sheer interest and perseverance. It takes practice - practice for the eye to learn to see, for the hand to duplicate what is seen. Everyone can learn to draw more accurately, but being a good drawer is not what art is all about. It is just one facet. We all need to remember that there are many arts that have nothing to do with realistic rendering...collage, sculpture, photography, ceramics, and jewelry design, to name a few.

Starting Points

Here are some drawing and painting approaches that you can suggest to get a child started:

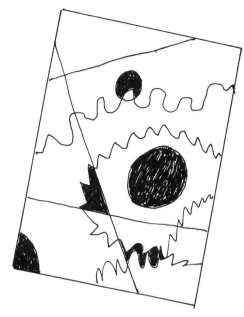

- Make a drawing with a black marker, and then color in between the lines, *filling the page* with colors.

- Try the reverse...make color shapes and then outline them.

- Draw some lines in black...simply abstract lines. Some may run off the page, some may make circles, some may connect to others, some may not touch any of the others. For fun, an adult can "dictate" a series of instructions for making lines, dots and circles. (*Example: "Draw a squiggled line from any edge of the paper, to any other edge of the paper...Then draw a circle that does not touch the line...Now draw a straight line that crosses the first line..."*) Some, or all, of the shapes and areas that are created by these lines are filled in with color.

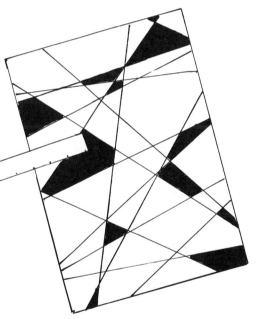

- Draw "scribbles" all over a page, and then fill in some of the spaces with color.

- Lay a ruler across a page...draw a line. Lay the ruler down again at another angle, and draw another line. Repeat this until there are lines all over the page. Then fill in the spaces with colors.

- "Draw" with glue, letting it dribble on the page. When it is dry, fill in with color. Try this on black paper with pastels or chalk for color.

- Work within a color limit *(See Color Limits, page 73, and Color, pages 35-37).*

- Fill the entire page with color...color not only the subject, but color the entire background too, all the way to the edge of the paper.

- Paint using a repeated image, creating a pattern. *(See About Patterns on page 88.)*

- Draw a "frame", a line or patterned border around the edge of the paper, with the subject in the center. Perhaps the border could include symbols or design elements that relate to the subject being framed.

- Make a patterned border, and then do a different pattern in the center.

- Outline your hand. Reposition it, and outline it again. Keep repeating. Allow it to overlap. Color it. Color the abstract shapes it makes by overlapping.

- Draw an outline of a person, and fill it with a pattern...then make the background another pattern design.

To Make Cardboard "Lifters":

Cut a piece of heavy paper or cardboard (index cards are perfect) to about 1¹/₂" wide by 4" long (A). Fold it on itself four times (B). Unfold it (C) and then form it into a square shape (D) and tape it (E). Glue this square lifter onto the back of a piece of cut out artwork (F), and then glue the lifter onto a prepared background. (G).

Now the artwork will be lifted from its background, to stand out three dimensionally (H). You will usually need more than one lifter, and some may need to be much narrower to accommodate smaller artwork.

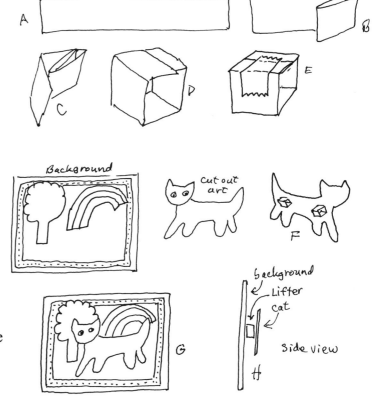

- Draw a frame or background. Then paint your subject on another piece of paper. When it is dry, cut it out and paste it on the frame or background. Try making it big enough to overlap the border...try pasting it on a folded piece of cardboard, a "lifter" (see facing page), to make it stand out from the background!

- After painting various subjects, cut them out and paste them in a new arrangement on colored paper.

- Paint, cut out and paste, just like above, but add pictures cut out from magazines, from direct mail catalogs, from gift wrap...

- Make a patterned background, using wallpaper scraps or gift wrap. Then paint or draw objects or figures, cut them out and glue them against the background.

Variation: Draw or paint the patterned background.

- Cut out a picture from a magazine or greeting card and glue it in the middle of a piece of drawing paper. Then "continue" the picture...add what the picture leaves out. If it is a picture of a monkey's face, draw the rest of the body, and give it a tree to sit in!

- Combine pictures and words...the words from a song, or a poem, or a name. Write the words in black ink, then color the page around them.

Variation: Write the words with white crayon and then color over them with watercolors.

Play With Pastels and Chalk

Take a piece of blank paper and just try some of these techniques...

Side Rubbing: Hold the pastel on its side and rub very lightly.

Soft Color: Put some color on the page. Rub it with a tissue. Use the tissue (that is now dusty with color) to smear color in another place. Or use your finger instead of tissue. This is a good way to cover large areas of color.

Bright Color Highlights: Spread some color with a tissue. Over this soft color take a bright color and scribble that color right over the soft color. (You'll see this done on the cover of this book.) Try different color combinations. Try a *light* color, such as yellow, over a *dark* color, such as purple.

Variation: Write the words with black marker, color the page with pastels, and then go back and touch up the letters with a metallic marker.

- Take letters of the alphabet and make them fanciful...turn a letter into an animal, or a flower, an insect, or a monster. Or distort and decorate them. This can be a good group project; everyone can combine their efforts to make the entire alphabet.

- Paint or draw showing an *emotion* with line and color.

  - Paint something strange...something surrealistic...something that doesn't make sense...something that startles.

  - Paint something using colors that are not normally considered "realistic" for it...a purple lawn, a pink horse, a yellow sky...

  - Paint something with an unusual *emphasis.* Perhaps you can exaggerate one of the objects, or contrast it, or highlight it.

  - Paint something from an *unusual point of view*...perhaps the basketball's point of view as it comes through a hoop, looking down at the players...or the point of view of an ant on a table...

- Paint or draw something with a strong light source...the bright sun, a lamp, a candle, the moon.

- Draw something without taking your eyes away from it...never looking at the paper.

- Paint the "negative" space, not the object itself.

- In pen and ink, or brush and black paint, experiment with shading by using stipple, wavy lines, cross hatch, squiggled lines, squares...make up your own.

- Paint something using flat, unshaded colors, none of the colors touching another, each color separated by the white of the paper.

Positive and Negative Space

When you draw an apple, that apple is considered the "positive" space in the drawing, while the space around it is the "negative" space.

- Draw using nothing but horizontal lines...or vertical lines...or dots...or with smudges of color.

- Draw with "reverse" perspective...objects get bigger as they recede.

- Draw with hierarchical perspective in a flat plane...the more "important" objects in the visual story are bigger, the less important objects are smaller.

- Do three drawings or paintings that are similar; they stand alone but together they make a set.

Color Limits

Color limits can open doors! Read about Color on pages 35-37, and try some of these:

- Use black and white only.
- Use black and white with shades of gray.
- Use black plus one color.
- Use black, a color, and that color's shades and tints.
- Use the three primary colors only.
- Use one primary and two secondary colors.
- Use two secondary and one primary color.
- Use black, one color, and its complement.
- Use two complementary colors, and their shades and tints.
- Use strongly contrasting colors.
- Use muted, related colors.
- Use warm colors (red, orange, yellow) with a cool accent.
- Use cool colors (purple, blue, green) with a warm accent.

What can I draw?

The thrilling exploration of color, shape and texture, *unbound by any subject matter,* is always a creative wellspring. But subject matter itself can also be a good launching point. And when a subject stimulates introspection and self-expression, the child learns something about art as a form of communication.

Dream Painting: Portray a dream you have had. (It can be a night dream or even a daydream.) Are you flying, riding a tiger, swimming with dolphins, driving a train, turning into an animal? What makes a painting look dreamlike?

Play With Paints

Learn painting techniques by experimenting with different ways to apply color...get out a blank sheet of paper and try these:

Graduated Wash: Load the brush with a paint color. Paint a solid area, moving the brush back and forth, down the page. Now add water to the brush, but don't add more color. Continue where you left off, still moving down the page. Add *more* water and continue. You'll see the wash (the area of color) get lighter and lighter.

Wet to Dry: Now do a wash, but instead of dipping the brush into more water or more paint, continue until the brush is dry, ending with a feathery effect.

Wet on Wet: Just like it sounds, this is when you paint an area with one color or with plain water, and then before it dries, load the brush with another color and paint in the wet first color. The second color bleeds into the first color with beautiful effects.

Dry Brush: Dip the brush into a paint color, and then brush off most of the paint on the palette. Now when you paint with it you get wispy brush strokes.

Double Loading: Load the brush with paint, and then dip the tip of it into a second color. Now paint with the brush loaded up with the two colors. Try holding the brush so it paints on the side of the bristles. Try loading three or four colors!

Now that you have a full sheet of paint experimentation, frame it if you like it as an abstract painting, or use it for another project! A collage, to make greeting cards (page 124), pins (page 132) or a Picture Weaving (page 90).

Flying High: If you could fly, *where* would you fly? To the top of a tree? To the moon? To the Amazon rain forest? To visit your cousins? Portray yourself flying there.

This Is Who I Am: Make a picture of yourself, your family, your pets.

Variation: Do your self-portrait while you study yourself in a mirror.

Variation for Older Children: Do a self-portrait using *symbols* of yourself. This could include colors, distinctive clothing, or objects you identify with, words from a poem that means something to you, or your hand print. It could even include your name as part of the design.

This Is Where I Live: Make a picture of your house, your street, your neighborhood, your school, your town. Portray a favorite place near where you live...a park, the beach, a pet shop, an ice cream store, a tree-lined street...

Home is Where the Heart Is: Portray what you love best about your home...a certain room, or a corner...perhaps an armchair, a window seat, or a secret hiding place in the garden. Or portray the whole house with all your favorite details lovingly exaggerated.

Dream House: Draw a bold outline of a house. Then fill it, and surround it, with all the things you'd love to have in your perfect fantasy house... big talking exotic birds, an indoor swimming pool, or a candy room with a gumball machine. Perhaps a house that is wild with vibrant colors...Or perhaps one that has a room for your very own tiger...

Feeding the Imagination: Create a colorful 3 dimensional table setting. Make a placemat and napkin by coloring white or colored paper, a plate by coloring a white paper plate. Create fantasy food (*see Play with Paper, page 79*) to glue on the plate. Cut out silverware from paper or foil. What else can you think of?

Fabulous Fauna: Paint an animal no one has ever seen before, one that you have made up. Give it a name. Write a story about it.

Ferocious Fauna: Paint a scary demon, made up out of your head. Where does it live? What does it eat? Give it a name, and write a story about it.

Picture the Season: Paint what you like about Spring, Fall, Summer or Winter. Paint your favorite part of a holiday or special annual family event.

Commemoration: Commemorate an event...a wedding, a new baby comes home, a family reunion...

Hero Worship: Make a picture of someone who is a hero to you...someone famous, or someone related to you...

Party Time: Make a picture of your most recent birthday party, a family party, a neighborhood block party, a wedding reception, a town celebration....

Caged Animals: Draw your favorite animal at the zoo, or aquarium. What does it like to do? What does it do best?

Animal World: Draw your favorite animal in its wild habitat. Who are its neighbors? What does it eat?

Circus Magic: Paint a picture of the circus. What is your favorite part?

Doing it Well: Make a picture of yourself doing something you enjoy doing...playing soccer, throwing a ball for your retriever, playing in an orchestra, doing art...

When You Are Drawing People...

- Try a side view
- Try overlapping people in a group
- Try drawing yourself, using a mirror set up next to you.
- Try drawing your own hand, your foot, your nose...
- Try drawing faces showing different emotions: sad, happy, angry...
- Try drawing whole figures showing these different emotions with their body language.

Someday: Make a picture of something you'd like to do when you're a grownup...piloting a space shuttle, conducting an orchestra, taking care of a sick animal, designing clothes, fighting forest fires...

For the Love of Books: Illustrate your favorite book. Draw your favorite character.

A Song on Your Mind: Make a picture of a song you like to hear, a song you like to sing.

Feelings: Paint how you feel about something that makes you feel very strongly...anger at a sibling, sadness about a friend moving, excitement about starting kindergarten...

Home Sick: Make a picture about how it feels to be sick, missing school, missing friends, missing out...

Scary Stuff: From monsters under the bed to earthquake, fire, flood, and abductions on the news...the world is full of things that frighten our children. When something has happened that particularly frightens your child, and you are talking about it together, you can encourage him to make a picture of it. This may not only help the child deal with his fears, but may also provide some illumination for you, helping you to see how he feels about them.

Cultural Values: If your family has a second culture, your child's art can be another way to maintain links with that culture. Make a picture that shows a traditional festival. Write out a song or poem in your language, and make a picture around it. Make a picture of yourself doing something (singing...dancing...praying...preparing food...) that is a part of that culture.

Variation: If your second language has a different alphabet, celebrate that alphabet by drawing it beautifully for a poster *(page 115)* or book *(pages 116-121).*

Our Spiritual Core: Art can be a way of reaching, exploring, and expressing our spiritual side. Religious values, experiences and community...these have been a rich source of subject matter for art during all of history.

Try Something New

Perhaps it is time to experiment with another medium. If your child has been doing a lot of marker drawing, get out a watercolor set. A lot of crayons? Suggest chalk on black paper.

Some children will enthusiastically plunge into something new...others may benefit from an introduction by an adult. But you do not need to be an artist to nudge a child into experimentation with a new medium. You can ask, "How are watercolors different from markers?...How are they similar?" Both of you can take a sheet of paper just for "fooling around" It doesn't matter what it looks like, it is just for experimenting. Try different brush strokes....dribble paint over the page... smooth a paint edge with a finger...overlay colors to get new colors...

Varying materials is not just for small children. If your older child has been working with colored pencils, introduce her to pastels or charcoal. If your teen likes oil painting, he might get excited about trying linoleum block printing.

There are other ways to vary materials. Encourage your child to try working with different kinds of surfaces, or try different ways to apply paint. Introduce a 4" wide brush, or sponges of different textures. Suggest painting with a feather, or grasses. Flick the brush to spatter paint. Use an eye dropper to dribble, drop and spatter paint. What kind of effect will you get when you dip string into paint and then drop it on the surface?

Surface Variety

What happens when you paint on these very different surface textures?

Smooth vellum paper
Heavy textured watercolor paper
Glossy coated paper
Brown wrapping paper
Gray cardboard
Black construction paper
Your own handmade paper

Collage

Whenever you glue something down onto paper or board, you've made a collage. Collages are one of the most inventive forms of art, and one that satisfies *any* age. Three year olds delight in sticking down colorful pieces of gift wrap and ribbon. An older teen will carefully cut apart magazine pictures and glue them down cleverly together to make a political statement. An adult will thrill to the rich combination of handmade paper and scraps of velvet...

Paper Versus Cardboard:

If you are working with paper collage, a paper base sheet is sufficient. If you are pasting objects, you will want a more substantial base. The corrugated cardboard with white on one side is an excellent low cost collage base.

Purely Paper

The simplest form of collage is paper on paper. The combinations, though, are *infinite*.

Plain Papers

Colored Paper: Cut up construction paper and glue the pieces down to make a picture. Do not use any drawing medium!

Variation: Tear the pieces of construction paper.

White on White: Make an abstract collage using only white and almost white papers, varying the texture and thickness of the papers. Handmade papers lend themselves to this. If you make your own *(see tin can paper making, page 82)* you can vary the thickness yourself.

Paper Mosaic: Tear or cut up papers of different colors into little shapes and make a mosaic out of them.

3-Dimensional Collage: Cut out pieces of paper and fold, twist, braid, crumple and bend them so they are not flat when they are glued onto the background.

Tissue Paper Collage: Tear or cut pieces of colored tissue paper. Pieces can be uniform squares, strips, or circles, or cut into interesting shapes...wavy, jagged or irregular. Where they overlap, the pieces blend their colors to make new colors. Brush with household starch for an adhesive.

See-Through Collage: Lay pieces of tissue paper down on waxed paper. Cover with another sheet of waxed paper. Put a sheet of plain paper under and over the waxed paper on your ironing board, and press with a warm iron. The wax melts, sticking the two sheets together. You can also add dried pressed flowers, threads, crayon shavings...

Printed Pictures Cutouts

Magazines, catalogs, greeting cards and gift wrap all provide a wealth of images to cut out and use in collages. You can cut out and use the image itself, or you can cut sections as abstract color blocks used for their overall color, instead of for their content. These can be combined with other color blocks to form a picture or design.

Strictly Collage: Cut or tear printed papers (magazine pages, gift wrap, newspaper) into many shapes and assemble them, trying to create a picture without any use of drawing.

Disjointed Creatures: Pictures of animals or people can be cut apart and reassembled in new forms. These make delightfully humorous and sometimes satirical pictures. A picture of an animal can be cut apart so its legs can be repositioned in exaggerated poses. The head of one creature can be put on the body of another. Entirely new - and often hilarious - species can be created this way. (Rainy days pass rapidly as deeply absorbed children pour through magazines to find just the right animal body...)

Mixed Media:

Drawing and Paper and Stuff: A picture, such as a self-portrait, can combine drawing or painting, with photos, pictures or blocks of patterned paper added to it. Ribbons, lace, string and other collage materials can be added.

Recycling Junk: Every household produces a wealth of materials for collage. String, ribbon, corks, lids and little boxes are just a beginning.

Nature's Bounty: Pressed flowers, dried grasses, twigs, leaves and seeds, tiny pebbles, shells and pinecones are lovely assembled into a collage.

Textiles: Fabric scraps, ribbons, lace, and string can be assembled for a textile collage. Try combining them on a cheesecloth background *(see below)*.

Kitchen Magic: Beans, rice and macaroni can be glued down on cardboard (or a paper plate) to make beautiful designs and textures. (Glued to little Styrofoam balls they make ornaments.)

Fine Materials: Handmade papers, marbled papers, metallic and cellophane papers, origami paper...these make elegant collages. Make your own paper *(see pages 82-83)* or marble your own *(see facing page)*. Add ribbon, raffia, old jewelry, lace, interesting artifacts...

Hanging: Make a wall hanging with one or two sticks and a piece of fabric. Sew or use fabric glue to make the fabric loop over at the top, to create a tunnel big enough to admit the stick. Tie on a cord hanger. With fabric glue, glue on fabric scraps, or natural things like pinecones, twigs, dried flowers...

Paste Versus Glue:

When you are working with odd shaped or heavy items (bottle lids, pinecones...) paste may work a bit more successfully than white glue. Paste will tend to hold the item even when wet, whereas white glue will not hold it until it is dry.

Background Magic...

For an interesting background texture, try dipping cheesecloth (available with cooking supplies) into a mixture of liquid household starch or white glue thinned with water. Lay it down on a piece of cardboard, and scrunch it into interesting folds.

Then go ahead and assemble the rest of your collage onto the cheesecloth, using more glue as you need it. When the cheesecloth dries, its gauzy folds will be set stiffly in place.

How to Marble Paper

Marbling paper is not collage, but it makes a wonderful collage material. You can also use it to decorate boxes, make jewelry, cover a book...

1. You'll need a wide high-sided tray or baking pan. Fill it halfway with water.

2. Mix some oil base paint with mineral spirits until it is quite diluted. Prepare several colors.

3. Dribble the diluted paint across the water. Swirl the water gently with a clean stick.

4. Lay a sheet of paper on top of the water (smoothing it to make sure the entire paper surface is in contact with the water.)

5. Carefully lift off the paper and lay it down to dry.

Tin Can Paper Making

Paper making is not a form of collage, but like marbled paper, handmade paper is a wonderful collage material. And both collage and the paper making process shown here involve recycling existing paper.

What you will need:

- A sink

- A blender

- A tray

- A sponge

- Two large cans (such as big coffee cans or large cookie tins). One of them (the smaller if they are not equal size) should be open at both ends. The other should be open at one end only.

- Screens - Several sheets of screen material, larger than the opening of the largest can. This can be metal screen, available by the yard at hardware stores, or the white plastic needlepoint grids available at needle craft and fabric supply stores.

- Paper - torn into small pieces (half inch to one inch pieces). Your paper can be white or colored, but it should not be coated (glossy) paper stock. Recycle school fliers, photocopy rejects, and art project paper discards (construction papers are excellent).

Tin Can Paper Making, continued

To make your paper:

1. Stack the two cans with the largest can on the bottom (this one is open at the top only), a sheet of screen on top of it, and the smaller can on top of that (this one will be open at both ends). See the drawing on facing page.

2. Put about a cup of loose paper pieces in the blender and add about a cup of water. (You will want to experiment with quantities to get the effects you want.) Blend until pulpy.

3. Pour the pulp into the top can. The water will run through into the bottom can, while the pulp will be caught by the screen.

4. After the water has drained through thoroughly, lift the screen off the can without touching the pulp. Set it on the tray and press it with a damp sponge to remove excess water.

5. Wait at least half an hour before trying to lift the pulp from the screen; then set it aside to dry.

Things to experiment with:

It is interesting to experiment with paper colors. It does not take much colored paper in the mix to add color to your paper pulp. Small amounts of paper colors that contrast with your main color can result in bright little specks of color.

Try adding bits of foil, threads, dryer lint, herbs and flower petals...these add interesting flecks in the paper. Try adding potpourris or essential oils for fragrance.

What to do with your paper:

- Use it in a collage.
- Use it as a background to mount a photo.
- Glue one or more pieces onto a folded card to make a greeting card. It can be enhanced with raffia, gold cord, a ribbon...
- Use a large, heavy piece as a book cover.

Duplicating an Image

We use all kinds of media to duplicate an image, and there is something for every age group. Simple stamps are easy for preschoolers. Sponge printing fascinates young children. Older children do beautiful things with block printing. Everyone loves the magic of rubbings and stencils.

Printing

It can be as simple as letting a preschooler paint her hand and then press it onto paper...it can be as complex as a three color lino block print. And if your older child doesn't want to stop there, then there are other printmaking techniques to move on to...such as lithography, silk screen, and photographic processes. These should be explored in classes, as they require special equipment and can be technically complex. Parents should also be aware that some of these, especially the photographic processes, require materials that can become quite expensive.

Direct Stamp Printing

Stuff and Gadget Printing: Time to experiment! Try using all kinds of household stuff as stamps. Dip crumpled paper into paint and use that to make marks on your paper. Dip a fork, a cork, some building blocks of different shapes...see who can come up with the most interesting household stamp!

Potato Stamp: Cut a potato in half. Carve a shape in the cut end, and trim away the background. Now you can press this into your stamp pad or a pool of paint in a paper plate and make patterns.

Sponge Stamps: Take household sponges and cut them into various shapes. Then dip them into paint and stamp them on the paper.

Leaf Stamps: Paint the backs of leaves and press them onto paper.

Variation: Paint the leaf backs with fabric paint, and press them onto a clean white T-shirt.

Offset Monoprints

A monoprint is a one-of-a-kind print, when you make just one printed impression from your prepared surface instead of multiple prints.

Bubble Prints: Very young children love bubble packing material...here's yet another use for it! Paint it and then lay paper on it to offset the impression onto the paper.

Glass Prints: Paint a piece of glass and then lay a piece of paper over the painted surface. Smooth it down to make sure it has made complete contact. Lift up the paper and it will have the painted picture offset onto it.

Variation: Lay out ceramic tiles in a group, about the size of the paper. Paint the tiles. You can paint a large, overall picture, like the glass print, or you can do something separate on each tile, to create a pattern effect. Lay the paper on the painted tiles, just as for the glass print, to make the monoprint.

Sandpaper Prints: Draw a crayon design on a piece of coarse sandpaper. Lay a piece of paper over the sandpaper and iron to transfer the image to the paper. (You must use crayon, because the wax transfers the color with the heat of the iron.) *Of course, young children should not handle the hot iron.*

Block Printing

With a cut block, you can make *many* impressions of the same design. Thus you can print the same image on a series of greeting cards, or repeat an image in a single large picture.

Styrofoam Prints: "Draw" a design on a piece of Styrofoam with a blunt pencil or ball-point pen, indenting the Styrofoam. Paint the surface and carefully lay a piece of paper over the Styrofoam. Smooth it to make sure the entire sheet of paper is in contact with the painted surface. Remove the paper and set it aside to dry.

About Registration:

When you are printing more than one color, you will need to find a way to line up the second color with the first, and place it exactly where you want it. This is called registration.

You have two parts to the registration problem. First, if you want more than one color (that cannot be applied at the same time to one block), you will need additional blocks cut for each color. These will need to *line up properly.*

Solution: Use light tracing paper to work up the design for each block. Mark the edge of the block on each sheet. Lay them over each other to verify that they line up correctly. Transfer each drawing to a separate block *(see page 57).*

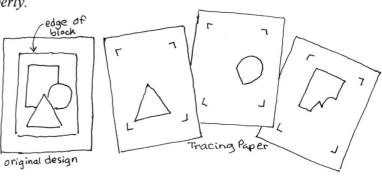

Second, when you print, each color block will need to be lined up so the color goes down just where you want it. But how can you see if the colors line up? The block covers the image area so you are working "blindly!"

Solution: When you print, mark the paper at the two top corners of the block with a very light pencil dot. Then each block can be lined up to those pencil dots. The dots can later be erased.

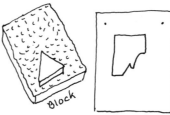

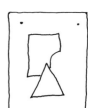

Wood or Linoleum Block Prints: Cut a design onto the block, and carefully lay paper over it to make your impression. Remove the paper and set it aside to dry. Because this process requires cutting with a sharp instrument, it should be limited to children who are old enough and mature enough to do this safely. *For more information on block printing, see page 58.*

Stenciling

Stenciling is not printing, but it is related because it too makes it possible to create multiples of one image. *(See About Stenciling on page 59.)*

Crayon Stenciling: Cut out a stencil and lay it in place on a piece of paper. Rub a crayon back and forth over the opening. When you lift the stencil, the shape will be there, in crayon. Try mixing lots of different colors together, and try different kinds of strokes...bold zigzag strokes, gentle coloring...

Variation: Pastels work beautifully with stencils. Again, experiment with color. Lay some color down and wipe it with tissue. Lay more down over that. Scribble or zigzag bright light colors over dark colors, dark over light...

Painted Stencils: Make your stencil, put it into place, and dab the open area with your brush. Sponge brushes are good for this. Make your own original stencils to decorate a box, a tabletop, a chair, a sisal rug, the walls of your room...

Variation: Use fabric paint to make stencils on T-shirts, jackets, hats, cushions, curtains....

Reverse Stencils

You can do "reverse" stenciling by laying down a shape, coloring over it, past its edges, and then lifting it up. Its shape will be left as the paper color.

This is an effective way to do lettering, using vinyl numbers and letters. *(See page 64).*

Stencil Cutting Tip:

Younger children have a difficult time cutting out a stencil. Encourage them to make their cut-out design very simple, and to *fold the paper first*, so when the cut is made, both sides are cut at the same time. Otherwise they will invariably cut from the edge of the paper. (When that happens, just tape it.)

About Patterns

A pattern is what you get when you plan a *repetition* of shapes, lines or colors, as you would with printing and stenciling.   Look around at fabrics, wallpapers, baskets...you will start to see patterns everywhere.   Here are some kinds of patterns:

The same shape can be used over and over, with the pattern formed by variations of color or size:

The same shape can be used over and over, but turned in two different directions:

◻◻◻◻◻◻◻◻◻◻◻◻◻

The elements can be alternating.

⌘⌘◻◻⌘⌘◻◻⌘⌘◻◻

The elements can be staggered.

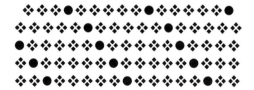

Different shapes can be used, that repeat themselves over and over in a predetermined order (this one prints a dark circle after every *five* sets of little diamonds.)

The elements can be changed *randomly* (by the toss of a coin, by the weather, by the artist's sense of balance...)

Try making your own sets of patterns. Generate a random pattern by tossing a coin (heads you print one of two elements, tails you print the other).

Rubbings

Another activity that is closely related to printing is making rubbings. You can duplicate an image by making additional rubbings of it.

Experimental Rubbings: Try making rubbings of many different things...some wild grasses, a piece of string, a coin, a leaf...Accumulate these things and then lay a piece of paper over each one, rubbing with a crayon. Try other media...oil pastels, colored pencils, a soft drawing pencil, charcoal. Play with color...try mixing colors as you rub so each item is more than one color. Try arranging some things for rubbing into a "picture", and make a final rubbing of them in your favorite medium.

Cardboard Rubbings: Cut out pieces of cardboard in many shapes and sizes. Stack two and glue them together. Place a piece of paper over them and rub with a crayon on the paper. The shapes will come through as a rubbing. Experiment with different combinations of sizes, shapes and stacks. Experiment by lining up the shapes into patterns so that the rubbing will be of a whole pattern at once instead of just one shape at a time. Experiment with different colors, making a rubbing using many colors. Try overlapping colors. Try this with other materials...colored pencils, oil pastels...

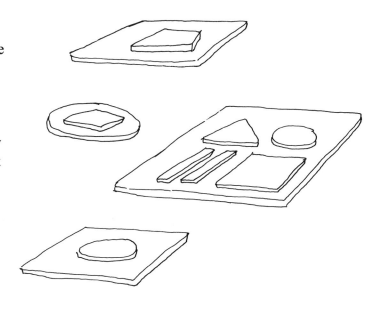

Styrofoam Rubbings: Make a design on the Styrofoam using a blunt pencil or ball-point pen, to indent it. Lay the paper over the Styrofoam, and rub with crayons, colored pencils or pastels.

Weaving

Traditional loom weaving is too complex to describe in this book, but there are some simplified weaving projects that are a lot of fun and produce wonderful results. The child who is very interested should be encouraged to learn more about weaving, through books and in weaving classes.

Paper Weaving: This is a weaving project that very young children can do successfully. Take a sheet of colored paper and fold it in half, (A). Make a series of cuts at regular intervals (1/2" or 1" apart) starting at the fold and stopping short of cutting through to the sides of the paper, (B). Choose another color, and cut strips of that paper. Weave the strips through the cuts, (C). Paste, staple or tape the ends of the strips.

Variation: When cutting the base page, make the cuts wavy instead of straight.

Variation: Weave flowers and grasses, instead of strips of paper, into the cut sheet of paper.

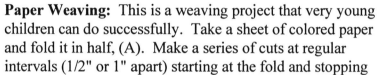

Picture Weaving: This is a project that gets surprising and sometimes very sophisticated results. It is the same as paper weaving, but uses two paintings or drawings instead of blank paper. These can be abstract or figurative, drawn for the weaving, or taken from the discard pile, but ideally they should have a lot of color coverage, not a lot of blank white expanse, and their colors should be different from each other.

Cut one of the pictures as in (A), above, and cut the second into strips, as in (B), keeping them in order. Weave the strips into the cut picture.

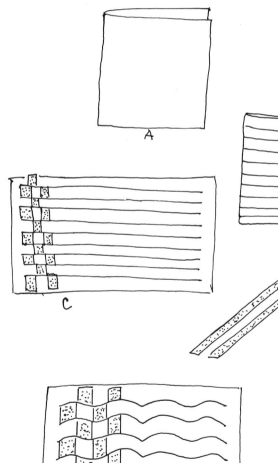

A Simple Lap Loom: A parent or older sibling can make a frame for a child using four pieces of wood about 1/2" thick.

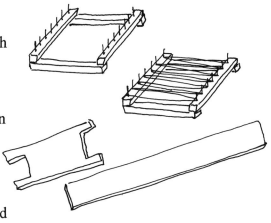

Line one side of the loom at measured intervals with finishing nails (the headless type) that are hammered in only about half way. Then match the other side. Tie a piece of string (this can be colored string to blend with the color of yarn being woven) on one of the top nails, and then loop it back and forth, *tautly*, to the last nail. Keeping it taut, tie it on the last nail.

Make a shuttle and shed stick out of cardboard or foam core. Tie the yarn to be woven at the beginning corner, and then wrap it around the shuttle. Weave the shed stick through the strings, alternating over and under. Turn it sideways to hold the strings apart. Slip the shuttle through the opening. Pull the yarn on its shuttle through the tunnel created by the shed stick. Do not pull too tight, or the sides will bow inward. Take out the shed stick and weave it through again, pushing it through the *other* direction, and this time *reversing* the over and under...where the first row went *over* a string, the second row will go *under*.

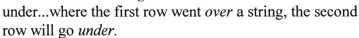

If you want stripe effects, change the colors of the yarn. When the piece is complete, tie the end piece of yarn to the last string end, and lift the piece off the loom.

Note: If the child is young, keep the size to about 6" square, and weave with the extra large yarns used for gift wrap; otherwise the project will take too long and will be frustrating.

Natural Hanging: Twigs, small pieces of driftwood, honeysuckle, wisteria and grape cuttings, ropes, strings, and raffia are materials that are worth a try in a natural hanging. Start with a larger horizontal piece such as a branch, or piece of driftwood. Tie a series of hanging materials from it. These should be flexible for weaving, such as rope or string. They can hang free, or be attached to a bottom piece. Weave other objects through the hanging, vertical, materials. Try weaving in twigs, driftwood, or feathers. Sometimes you can find seashells with holes in them that you can tie to the hanging.

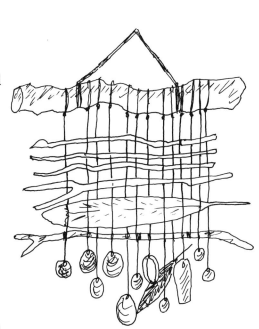

Sewing

All too often we tend to think that sewing is just for older kids. But some children as young as five can learn to operate a sewing machine, and at that age they are more open to experimentation, less afraid of imperfection, and far less concerned with gender bias, than they will be later. At a young age children can certainly make costumes (capes, skirts), drawstring bags (for marbles, for jewelry), and pillows (for themselves, for their teddy bears, for the family cat). These simple projects are "forgiving"...they can be successfully made by the uninitiated (with some help from an adult, who needs only minimal sewing skills in order to follow the directions), and they provide a lot of latitude for creativity.

With the skills developed by starting at an early age, by the time a child reaches ten he can go on to make such things as hats, vests, tote bags and quilts. Eventually, teenagers who have been sewing for some time can not only design and make their own clothes, but can make beautiful and creative gifts for others, at a fraction of the cost of ready-made.

Most of these sewing projects will need some use of a hot iron. Young children, of course, will need help with the ironing.

Dress-up Scarves: Cut pieces of light fabric, some long and narrow, some in big squares.   Hem each one by folding over the edge about 1/4", pinning the fold, and sewing it. This kind of finishing does not compare to a hand rolled scarf edge, but it will hold up fairly well with the wear and tear of the world of pretend.

Dream Pillow: Children are enchanted by the idea of sleeping with a pillow that will help bring them wonderful dreams. A dream pillow can

be snuggled with, talked to, even confided to at night. Some kids share the pillow with a doll or a teddy bear. But it is most treasured when they make the pillow themselves.

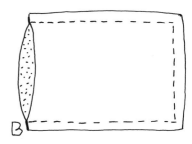

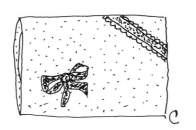

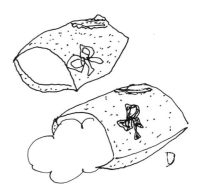

You will need a very small amount of fabric (fabric scraps will usually suffice) and pillow stuffing (available at fabric stores).

Cut two pieces of fabric the same size each (6" x 8" is a good size). You can use two pieces of the same fabric, or use a different fabric each side. Hand sew any decorations that will go on it, such as ribbons, bows, sequins, rickrack (gold is popular) or buttons (jeweled buttons are highly prized.) Be sure to sew the decorations on the right side of the fabric! (A)

Then pin the fabric together, wrong side out and right sides together. Sew the pillow on three sides (B). Turn it right side out and press (C). Stuff with pillow stuffing (D).

Finally, pin the open side shut, and stitch it.

Variation: Use white cotton fabric, and then paint it with fabric paints. Paint the pieces *before* sewing them together, or *after* sewing three sides, turning it right side out, and pressing it.

Bean Bag: Follow the pillow instructions, only make it smaller. You can make any shape you wish, just so both pieces of fabric are cut to the same shape. When you sew the three sides, also sew most of the fourth side, leaving an opening just large enough to insert your filling. Turn right side out, press, and fill with dried beans, popping corn, rice or lentils. Then stitch the opening shut.

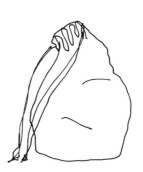

Drawstring Bag: Such a useful bag! It can hold sports gear, ballet shoes, doll clothes, school lunches, a rock

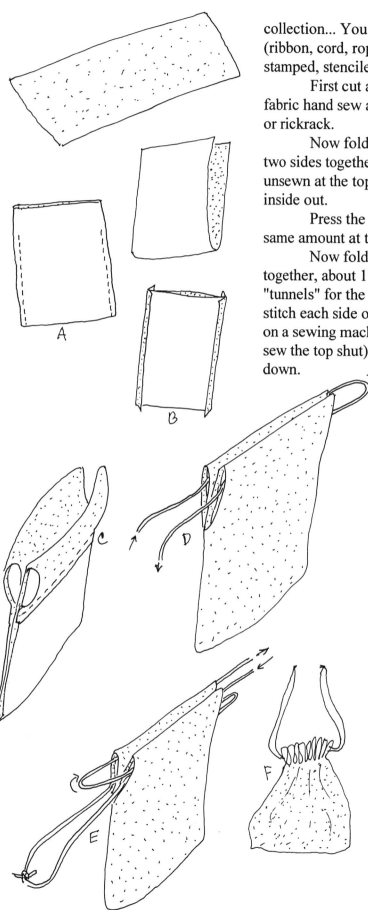

collection... You will need fabric and drawstring material (ribbon, cord, rope). It can be personalized with trim, or stamped, stenciled or painted with fabric paints...

First cut a long rectangle. On the *right* side of the fabric hand sew any decorations, such as buttons, ribbons, or rickrack.

Now fold the rectangle in half and pin and sew the two sides together, *right sides together,* but leave about 2" unsewn at the top on each side (A). The bag should now be inside out.

Press the seams open, including turning back the same amount at the top 2" where it is not sewn. (B)

Now fold down each top half, again wrong sides together, about 1" (C). This will form two separate "tunnels" for the drawstring, one on each side. Pin and stitch each side of the top separately. This will be difficult on a sewing machine for the younger kids (they are likely to sew the top shut) so they may want to hand stitch the tunnel down.

Turn the bag *right*-side out and press it. *You may need to hand stitch the side where the side seam meets the tunnel.* Now you are ready to thread the cord through the tunnels.

Take two pieces of cord, both the same length, each about twice the width of the bag. Pin a large safety pin to one end of the drawstring material and push it through the first tunnel. Keep pushing the safety pin through, scrunching the fabric along the drawstring material. When the safety pin emerges at the end of the first tunnel, poke it into the second tunnel and thread back to where you started (D).

Now start at the other side of the bag, and thread a second cord through the opposite way. When you have threaded both cords through, you will have two drawstrings, a set coming out of each side (E). Knot each cord *to itself.* Now when you pull on both strings at the same time the bag will shut tight (F).

94

Cape: A cape is easy to make, and can be many costumes, depending upon the fabric. For instance, it can be an elegant black velvet cape, a pink satin princess cape, or a blue Superman cape (the red and yellow "S" can be cut out of felt and glued into place with fabric glue.)

Measure the child to determine the desired length of the cape and add two inches. The width should be about that of the child's arm span, with arms held outstretched. This gives you the minimum size of the piece of fabric that you will need. You will also need ribbon or cord to tie the cape.

First hem the fabric piece by turning all four sides over $1/4$", wrong sides together. Pin and stitch. *(Exception: if one of the edges is the "selvage", the machine finished edge of the fabric, that edge does not need to be hemmed.)*

Take the side that will be across the shoulders, and turn the fabric over *again,* wrong sides together, about $1 1/2$" (A). Pin and stitch this to make a "tunnel" for the tie cord. When you have made the tunnel, there will be an opening at each side of the cape for the cord (B). Attach a safety pin to the cord material, and thread it through the tunnel.

Scrunch the fabric along the tie cord to gather the fabric to the desired amount. Make sure the ties are hanging down in even lengths. While the cape is gathered, stitch the ends of the tunnels to the ties (C) so that the cape does not become ungathered again.

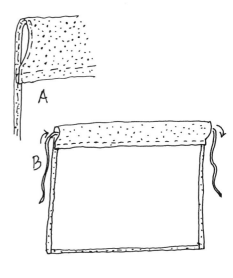

Easy Skirt: Like the cape, the skirt can be many things...it can be made in white netting to be a ballerina's skirt, pink satin lining fabric to be a princess skirt, flowery chintz to be an "old fashioned" skirt...use your imagination!

Before you start, measure the child to determine the desired length of the skirt and add three inches. Measure the child around the waist, multiply that by three, and add two inches. That is roughly the minimum size piece of fabric you will need. You will also need waistband elastic, a couple of inches longer than the waist measurement.

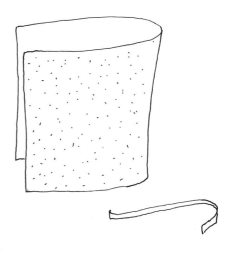

95

Fold and pin the fabric, *right sides together,* and sew up the side seam (A). With the skirt still *inside out,* fold down the waist about ¼", wrong sides together, and stitch it. Fold it down again, about 1½", pinning it in place and stitching all the way around the waist to make a "tunnel" (B).   You will have to leave about an inch unstitched, however, so you have a place to insert the elastic (C).

Attach a large safety pin to the elastic and thread it through the "tunnel" (D). When complete, temporarily pin the elastic with the safety pin, *estimating* the waist tightness.

Turn the skirt *right side out* and press. Try on the skirt. Adjust the tightness of the elastic until it is comfortable and safety pin it in place again. Hand stitch the elastic, remove the safety pin, and trim the excess elastic. Hand stitch the one inch opening to the "tunnel".

Check the length. It should be within an inch of the right length. Turn the hem under about ¼", *wrong sides together*, pin and stitch. Then turn the hem up another ¾" and stitch it.   Decorate it with trims, buttons, fabric paint...

Variation: Use a plain colored cotton fabric and then stamp, stencil or paint it with fabric paints. Sometimes it is easier to paint the fabric before you start sewing.

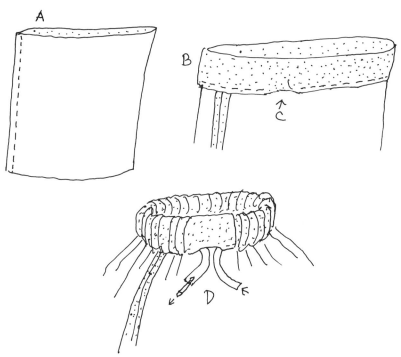

Constructions

Constructions are somewhere between collage and sculpture. Not only are their creative possibilities endless, but for some children constructions can be an appealing introduction to art. In fact, constructing things out of wood, Styrofoam and boxes, using hammer, nails and glue, can make an artist out of the child who may think he *has* no interest in art.

Sculpture and Constructions present an interesting challenge to children. No longer is there just a flat picture plane to think about, for they are generally viewed from many, or even all angles. There are also some structural concepts to master, to learn *how* to make the piece stable by forming a solid base and figuring out supports.

A particularly useful material for constructions is the Styrofoam used by manufacturers to pack their merchandise. Some are simply blocks, but many are in intriguing shapes that are just waiting to be used in constructions.

Box City: On a large board or sheet of foam core, assemble a city made up of boxes for buildings. They can be painted or covered with papers. Paint the street, lawns, sidewalks. (The child with a matchbox car collection will have a wonderful time filling the streets with vehicles, and adding garages, parking lots and repair shops.) This is a good group activity. *(For more variations on this kind of project, see "Environments", page 105.)*

View Boxes: Take any box, such as a shoe box, and turn it on its side. Paint a scene inside. Glue things inside. It could be an underwater scene, with shells and sand glued in place. It could be a household scene with family members drawn, cut out of paper, and glued in place. It could be the outdoor garden adjacent to a dollhouse.

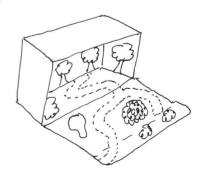

Bathtub Boat: Make a boat using a piece of wood with things nailed on it...lids, spools, large beads.

Clock: Anyone can make a clock, but younger children will need some assistance. Before you start, purchase your clock assembly. This is the little battery-operated mechanism with the hands for the face of the clock (available at craft stores.) You will need this in advance to be sure your center hole will accommodate the hands, and to know how long the hands are.

Before you start, *plan* your clock. Make a sketch on a piece of paper the same size as the material you plan to use for the clock face. Measure how far the hands will extend. Older children may want to plan the clock face, how it will be painted, what will be glued on it...what colors, what design, what you will use for numbers. And don't forget to plan a way to hang or stand the clock.

If you are using wood, trim it to your final shape if necessary. Drill the center hole for the mechanism. Sand it carefully, and then varnish it or paint it with white primer and then colored paint if you like, and glue on decorations. If you are not happy with the color of your purchased "hands", you can prime and paint them as well. Let your imagination go wild!

This is something that will be enjoyed for a long time, so make it durable. (A glue gun may be helpful.) You probably will want to give the finished piece a clear protective coating before slipping the clock assembly through the center hole from the back, and attaching the hands to the front.

Abstract Sculpture

Styrofoam Creations: Glue together some Styrofoam packing forms to make an interesting shape. A glue gun may be helpful. The final sculpture can be painted with tempera or acrylic paints, and given a protective coating.

Foam Core Building Blocks: Cut up foam core (1/2 thick is best, but thinner pieces will work) into many shapes and sizes...6" squares, 2" squares, big and little rectangles, long skinny strips, triangles, arches. An adult should do this cutting for young

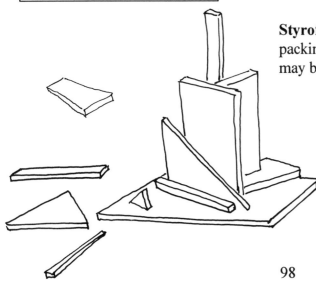

children. The child can put them together to form a structure, a sculpture, gluing the pieces together. It can be left white (a very dignified, austere piece) or painted.

Airy Wire with Color: Take coat hangers and open them with pliers. If this project is for younger children, an adult should prepare the hangers by bending each end with pliers until it is almost closed (A). This makes it easier for children to hook the ends onto the other sections of wire.

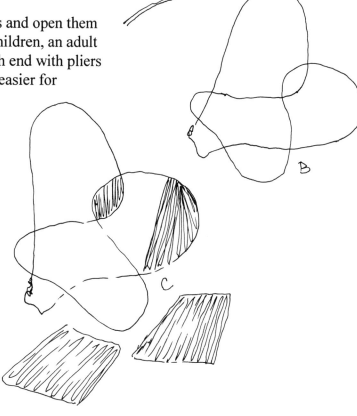

Bend the hangers into shapes, hooking as many hangers together as you like (B). Then choose colored tissue paper, cut a piece to size, brush it with liquid starch, and place it over the wire so it covers an open space between wires. Now that *open space* has become a *colored shape.*(C) Fill in the sculpture with as many pieces of tissue paper as you like. Try playing with colors, putting more than one color in each area. Mix a color with its complement, or put two warm colors together. *Note: Wear old clothes and work over a tray. The tissue paper colors tend to run.*

Found Objects Assemblage: An assemblage is an art form where objects originally intended for other uses are used in a piece of art. Junk can be put to good use in this kind of sculpture. A big piece of rusty metal can be a starting point...put it on a base, add other things to it. The whole thing can be left rusty, or even sanded, primed and painted...perhaps a bright primary color!

Mobiles

A mobile is not only a hanging sculpture...but one that can move!

Coat Hanger Mobile: This is an easy first mobile for the preschooler. Cut pieces of cardboard into different shapes...freeform or shapes. Punch a hole in the top of each

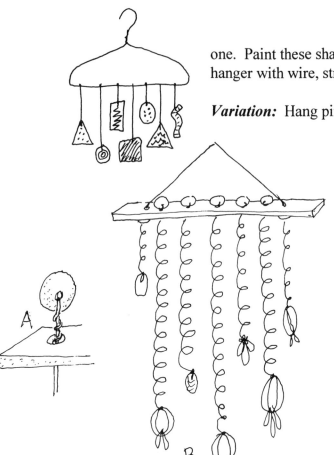

one. Paint these shapes and then hang them from a coat hanger with wire, string or fishing line...

Variation: Hang pinecones, shells, other found objects...

Spring Mobile: Drill holes in a piece of wood or driftwood. Pull springs open until they are stretched out of shape, long and bouncy. Or coil some heavy wire to make it like a loose spring. Hang these pieces of springy wire from the piece of wood. You can just tie the wire through the holes, but if you have some large beads, try using them to anchor the wire. Simply put the wire through the bead and then back down to twist on itself (A). The beads, being bigger than the drilled hole, will hold the wire. Hang interesting objects at their ends (B)...such as shells, painted juice concentrate lids, oven fired clay medallions *(see page 103). (Note: You'll find that objects that are too heavy will pull the bounce out of the wire.)*

Airy Mobile: Make two or three of the wire and tissue sculptures described on page 99. Then take a matching coat hanger and instead of pulling it apart, leave the hook at the top and simply cut the wire on the bottom of the triangle. (Don't cut it right in the middle...it will be more interesting if one side is longer than the other.) Then attach the wire sculptures to the ends, making a mobile.

Totem Mobile: Gather everyday objects...plastic fruit, little dolls, toy planes, forks...they can make a delightfully quirky mobile. Start by making a wooden hanging frame by nailing two pieces of wood (1"x1") at right angles (or you can use just one piece of wood) and drilling small holes along the wood. Some holes will be for rope or wire going up to hang the mobile. The rest of the holes will be for wire or rope going down, to hang the objects. Pass the thin rope or wire through the hole and tie a knot to secure it (or use beads as described above). Add the objects to the mobile *as it hangs* (so you can keep it balanced).

Clay

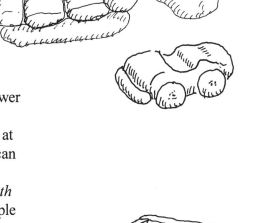

Some clay projects must be fired at high temperatures in kilns, while others can be hardened at lower temperatures. If you use clays that are fired in your household oven, your child can create all kinds of things at home. For the lucky few with access to a real kiln, you can explore glazed ceramics. Whether you use home fired modeling clay, or kiln fired clay, please read *Working with Clay*, on the next page, which describes some of the simple clay techniques of pinch, coil and slab.

Of course your child will enjoy making little bowls, little animals, people, even cars, but the following are a few other options.

Clay House: Using slabs, make a cabin, a little house, a castle. *Tip: Cut the windows and doors before assembling.*

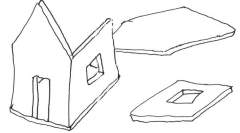

Tableau: Make little figures and place them on a slab... perhaps in a structure like a house open on one side. Tell a story with the tableau..

Hanging Tile: Make a slab tile, decorated with stamped or scratched designs, and punch one or two holes at the top with a straw. Hang it with a leather thong, raffia, rope or silk cord.

Mosaic Tiles: Cut little tiles from a slab. Fire, paint or glaze them, and then assemble them as a mosaic, gluing them to a board, a piece of foam core, or a larger slab of fired clay.

Try this...

Press leaves into your ceramic clay piece. They will dissolve into ash when fired, leaving their beautiful impressions behind.

Working with Clay

These three techniques are helpful for getting children started with any kind of clay, whether it is play dough, modeling clays, air-dried, oven-dried, or ceramic clays.

Pinch Pots: This is the simplest way to make a small pot or figure. Start with a ball of clay, and simply pinch it into shape.

Coil Method: Roll "ropes" of clay and then coil them up on a flat slab base to form sides. Keep coiling more "ropes" to make the desired shape, pinching the coils together as you go. Smooth them by rubbing with the back of a spoon. *(Note: To make large ropes, for larger pots, squeezing the clay may be easier than rolling.)*

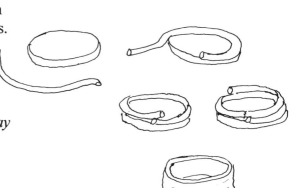

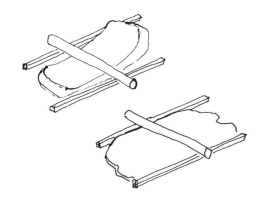

Slab Method: Roll clay out into flat pieces that are uniformly thick. One way to produce a uniform thickness is to lay two sticks on either side of the clay. Then rest the dowels on the sticks as they roll the clay. The size of the sticks will determine the thickness of the clay. For a small thin slab, you could even use pencils.

Another way to prepare slabs is to take a hunk of clay and pound it into a large mound, then cut slabs out of this with your clay cutting wire.

Allow some time for the slabs to loose some of their moisture and firm up before being used. Then they can be trimmed and joined together to form all kinds of pots, bowls, houses and boxes.

To join them together, rough up the surface of the joining sides with a nail or a fork, and then wet those sides with slip (water softened clay). The slip will act as an adhesive.

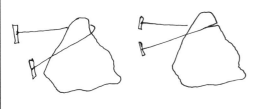

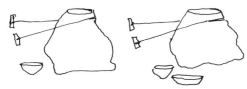

Clay Beads: Make beads of all shapes...round, oval, square...punch a hole with a straw or tooth pick, and then fire and glaze or paint them. If you are working with pre-colored oven fired clay, you won't have to paint them.

Variation: Make a larger, flatter shape. Put a hole in it to become a hanging medallion, or glue it to a barrette or pin backing.

Multi-colored Beads: Using *pre-colored* oven fired clay, roll long tiny strands of various colors. Bundle them together, and then slice through them to get a cross-section of color. Then roll it, or twist it, to get multi-colored beads. Play with many different color combinations.

Variation: Use thinly sliced cross sections of the unfired bundled colors to decorate an unfired bowl made of the same clay, or to cover a clay medallion. Then fire the covered piece.

Plaster of Paris Plaque: This is not a clay project, but it is similar, and very young children love it. Prepare plaster of paris *(see page 32).* Leave it white or tint it with powdered tempera or food color. Pour it into a form...a round plastic lid or the bottom of a square milk carton will do. Decorate by placing things in it while it is still soft...beads, shells, pinecones, buttons. Or press a hand print into it. When it is firm, remove it from the form. *Remember, do not allow any liquid plaster of paris to get anywhere near your drains. Pour excess plaster into a throwaway container.*

World of Pretend

In this section we will be looking at ideas that are not really what we *normally* call art...but this is an important part of the creative process, nonetheless. When children get in the habit of making things early on - instead of being passive recipients of entertainment - they just seem to keep on making more and more as they grow up. It's a habit that snowballs. The child who made doll clothes is more likely to one day tackle the design of her own clothes. The child who made his own cardboard race car is more likely to one day be inventing things with motors. It's up to us as parents to turn off the TV and encourage them, when they are young, to not only do art but to *make their own entertainment.*

Play Props

Young children love to play house, to play school, to play store. Instead of buying ready-made "kitchens" for them, encourage them to make their own stove on a box by drawing burners on top (turned on its side, the flaps could be the door to the oven). A shoe box can be a cash register, with numbers and buttons drawn all over it. (And "money" can be drawn on pieces of paper and stored inside the box.) Another box can have a screen drawn on one side, with keys and buttons, becoming a computer.

Dress-up can be as simple as some scarves and capes. Jewelry? Children can make their own by stringing buttons, cut up straws, or macaroni. Face paint is fun, especially for special occasions, such as a pretend theater

Make Your Own Face Paint

You will need for each color:
1 teaspoon cornstarch
1/2 teaspoon cold cream
1/2 teaspoon water
Food coloring
Cotton swabs to apply paint

In a muffin tin, mix each color in a separate well. Stir cornstarch and cold cream until well blended. Add water and stir. Add food coloring one drop at a time.

Apply with cotton swabs, keeping face paint away from eyes. Wash off with soap and water.

presentation or circus. Make your own, or use aquarelles (they wash off with water.)

Environments

Take a cardboard box and make it a dollhouse, a mouse manor, a snail castle, or a monster lair. Make a paper mache world of hills, ponds and roads. Design your dream house. Make an architectural wonder.

Paper Mache Miniature World: There are all kinds of environments that kids can make for their favorite toys. With paper mache you can fashion hills, caves, water, and beaches, creating a little world for some tiny plastic animals, a road system for matchbox cars...

Take a piece of foamcore or wood (the foamcore will be easier to handle) and mark lightly in pencil roughly what your plan is...where you will put a road, a hill, a lake. Crumple paper and tape it down to form the contours of the land. A hill will need a big pile of crumpled papers. Start putting strips of paper mache *(see page 33)* on the contours. Build it up and create any textures you want. When it is dry, paint it. You can sprinkle sand on wet paint to create a sandy texture, and glue pebbles and twigs in place. When the creation is complete, give it a protective coating.

*Storage
Tip:*

Measure the clearance under your child's bed, and plan your environment to be low enough to fit!

One Room Doll House: A 24" cardboard box accessed from the top can be a one room house for a Barbie or a Ginny doll. A shoe box will make a charming house for a two inch toy mouse. Polly Pocket may feel more comfortable in an even smaller box.

Cut windows and doors (an adult should do the cutting) and use fabric or lace scraps to make curtains. Use gift wrap or wall-paper scraps to paper the walls, fabric to carpet the floor (velvet works as a lovely rug in a tiny house). Make tiny paintings to hang on the walls. Make tables and chairs from boxes covered with fabric or paper, or use spools for tables in very tiny houses.

Dollhouse Conversion: Many girls, when they get to be about nine years old, long for a fancy dollhouse, a step up from the machine made, machine printed metal or pasteboard house. They want to decorate the house, rather than accept the walls and floors that have been printed by the

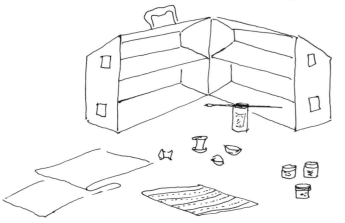

manufacturer. But the lovely big wooden dollhouses, even when sold as kits, are expensive, out of reach for many.

An alternative is to pick up one of the machine made houses at a garage sale or second hand shop, and spray paint it with white primer. Then your child can personalize it by painting it herself. She can paper the walls with printed paper (gift wrap, wallpaper), and install velvet carpeting...

Variation: Take one of the smaller metal fold-out houses made for younger children, paint it with white primer, and transform it into a charming mouse house, complete with mouse-sized furnishings...spools, thimbles, and walnut shell baskets. (For inspiration, look at the books by Beatrix Potter or Jan Brett.)

Architectural Wonders: Construct a three dimensional building...a fairy castle...a space creature's palace...or simply a beautiful architectural shape. Perhaps with towers, perhaps with columns, out of Styrofoam, wood

scraps, boxes, wire, spools...nailed and glued. Decorate with shells, paper, paint...

House Model: Older children may be interested in making a more sophisticated model of a house, perhaps designing their "dream house". This takes careful planning and some layout drawings. Pieces of foamcore can be cut carefully to the plan of the drawings, and glued together, just as architects do for real design models.

Dolls and Animals

Dolls are a source of much enjoyment and creative play. They are a wonderful opportunity for a child to "act out" different roles and scenarios, whether with a fancy lady doll with a porcelain head or a comfy plush bear, a two inch furry mouse or a Barbie doll. They can be the source of even more creativity if your child learns to make clothes and other accessories for her doll. There are even some dolls your child can make.

Paper Dolls: Invent your own people, with all their fine clothes! First draw the outline of the doll carefully in pencil on stiff paper or light cardboard. (Many children prefer to draw the figure first on another piece of paper and then transfer the outline to the final paper or cardboard. *For transferring, see page 57.*) Then color the figure and cut it out. To draw clothes that will fit this doll, set the cut

out paper doll on white paper and *lightly* outline its figure in pencil. Then draw the clothing, in pencil first, to fit the figure. Don't forget to add tabs, especially at the shoulders, to hold the clothes on the figure. Go over the clothing outline with pen, and erase the light pencil outline of the doll's figure. Color in the clothes, and cut them out (being especially careful while cutting the tabs.)

Sock Pony: Take a large sock, cut 3" off the cuff, and set this piece of ribbing aside. Stuff the sock with pillow stuffing (or old nylon stockings) and attach it to a broom handle with duct tape. Sew button eyes (7/8" buttons are a good eye size.)

Now for the ears. Take the piece of sock ribbing you have set aside, and cut it along the ribs into two pieces. Lay one of the pieces in front of you with the *finished* edge of the ribbing on top (A). Starting at one of the corners, loosely stitch along all three cut edges, leaving the finished edge unstitched (B). Pull on the thread to gather it tightly and knot it (C). Then sew this ear in place (D) and make the second ear using the other piece of ribbing.

Tip:

Kids tend to draw small figures. Encourage your child to draw the paper doll at least 6" or 8" tall by providing a top and bottom mark on the sheet of paper. *Smaller dolls are more difficult to work with.*

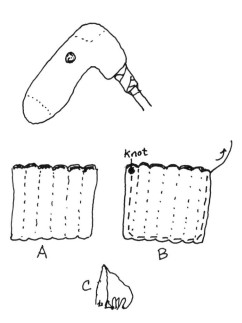

107

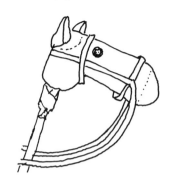

Make a bridle out of brown seam binding, available at fabric stores. *Optional:* Embroider a "star" on the horse's forehead; sew a yarn mane onto the forehead and neck.

Pillowcase Dolls: You can use an old pillowcase, or make your own fabric bag, sewn three sides, to start. Crumple some newspaper tightly into a ball and place it inside the pillowcase, at the center of the closed end. Tie a cord around it, on the outside of the pillowcase, to make a head. Tie two pieces of cord around the two pillowcase corners, to make arms. A face can be drawn with markers or fabric paint.

Spoon and Clothespin Dolls: This is a charming children's project from yesteryear that very young children will be thrilled to make, using little wooden ice cream spoons and old fashioned one-piece clothespins. (These can still be found, in craft stores and sometimes in old fashioned dime stores.) With a marker draw a face and glue on string or yarn for hair. Little glue-on movable eyes, available at craft stores, are fun. Then wrap the doll with fabric, or draw clothes directly on.

Doll Clothes: Barbie dolls spend much of their time changing clothes. A lot of money can be spent on their wardrobes, without exercising much creativity. On the other hand, much of their clothing is fairly easy to duplicate, modified with a child's own colors and designs.

Carefully examine an article of Barbie clothing and ask a few questions. Does it require stretchable fabric or regular fabric? Turn it inside out. How many seams does it have? Lay it on a piece of paper and trace its shape, allowing a little extra for the seams.

Use the drawing to cut the same shape out of a fabric scrap and stitch it together by hand. Add interesting trim, little buttons, sequins. Use Velcro or snaps for fasteners.

Now all you'll need to buy are the plastic high heels. (Tip...a little tiny piece of silly putty in the toes of the shoes will keep those darn things on Barbie's feet.)

Tiny Feasts: Barbie dolls, Ginny dolls, clothespin dolls, furry mice dolls...they all have to eat. Use oven-fired clay to make little plates and platters of food.

108

Puppets

Puppets are a wonderful activity for a group of children. Siblings can design their own puppets, and plan a puppet play. The "only" child can make extra puppets for when friends come to play.

Paper Bag Puppets: Use small paper bags, perhaps a maximum of 5" wide, because they are easier for a child to manipulate. White bakery bags are good because colors show up well on them. On the other hand, brown bags are closer to natural skin color. Color a face on the base of the bag, with the mouth at the edge where it tucks against the side. This way the fingers inside the bag can make it open and close its mouth.

Sock Puppet: Take an old sock, and sew button eyes on it. Fold the sock where the mouth will be, and stitch the sides of the mouth. An enterprising child can embroider lips!

Fabric Painted Puppet: Cut the puppet shape, bigger than the child's hand, on two thicknesses of white fabric. Sew the two pieces together, right sides together, leaving the bottom open. Turn it right-side out and press. Now the child can paint the face, hair and clothing with fabric paints.

Paper Mache Puppet: This puppet offers a wide range of character and expression. *(Note: Young children may lose interest during the somewhat lengthy process of layering and working the paper mache.)*

To start, crumple newspapers tightly into a ball, roughly the size you want for the puppet's head. Keep in mind, however, that a head larger than 3" in diameter may be a bit top heavy to easily support on one finger.

Take a toilet paper tube and hold it to the newspaper ball. Tape it in place with masking tape (A).

Follow the instructions for making Strip Paper Mache *(page 33)*. Layer the strips over the newspaper ball and down over the tube where it meets the head. Apply layer after layer, until the surface is fairly uniform (B). You can pinch the paper mache to make features. You can also make some Pulp Paper Mache *(page 33)* to make a final

coating that can be shaped into facial features. If you do, you will want to let the strip layers dry first.

Allow the paper mache to dry thoroughly. This will take days.

While the head is drying, you can make the fabric body. It will be very much like making a Fabric Painted Puppet *(page 109)* but it will not include a head. Instead, make a neck that will be wide enough (allowing for side seams) to fit around the paper tube. In fact, be generous with the size overall. You do not need to use white fabric and fabric paints - you can use a patterned or plain colored fabric for the body.

When you sew the sides together (right sides together), leave the neck and bottom open (C). Double check that the neck is just wide enough to admit the tube. Turn the body right side out and press it (D).

When the paper mache head is dry, paint the face and hair. When the paint is dry, give the head a clear protective coating. If you like, you can glue yarn or fabric fringes on the head to be hair. Fabric fringes are easier for younger children. Cut a strip of fabric, and then make a row of cuts in it that do not go all the way across (E). Then glue these strips (or yarn) in *rows*, starting at the lower hairline near the neck, and overlapping them, row by row, up to the center part at the top of the head (F).

Push the tube through the fabric neck opening. To glue it in place, turn the fabric inside out, over the puppet's face. Trim the excess cardboard tube, and glue the tube where it meets the neck fabric.

Masks

Paper Plate Masks: Cut eye holes, a mouth hole, and a breathing flap (see drawing) in the paper plate. Decorate the plate with feathers, glitter, paint... Rubber bands can be looped to each side, to go over the ears. Otherwise, a stick handle can be glued to the bottom so the mask can be held in front of the face.

Paper Mache Balloon Masks: Inflate a balloon. Cover it with strip paper mache *(see page 33)*, in several layers so it will be thick and sturdy when dry. When it is dry, cut out the back, but do not cut away the top of the head (this helps the mask stay on, because it can rest on the child's head). Put it on the child to mark, with pencil, where you will cut eye, mouth and breathing holes. Attach elastic or a rubber band at the sides. Paint and decorate the mask.

Optional: After cutting eye, mouth and breathing holes, you can build up these and other features using pulp paper mache (page 33). Let it dry thoroughly before painting.

Tip:

Don't just make one mask... do a series. As you get the hang of the process, you will do more and more interesting things with them. Then display them as a group on the wall.

Game Time

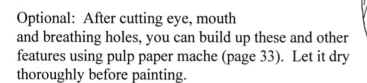

Children can make up their own board games. To start, they may want to pattern their games off another game they already know, such as Candy Land, or Chutes and Ladders. They can make their own folding board *(see below)*. They can even make movers with oven fired modeling clay.

Chess fans will enjoy making their own chess pieces out of clay, either ceramic or oven fired. (If ceramic, make plenty of extra pieces because accidents tend to happen during the hot firing process.)

Folding Game Board: Take a piece of cardboard the size you want the final board to be, and cut it in half. Lay the two pieces side by side where they will hinge. Temporarily tape them with masking tape so they are about 1/4" apart.

Carefully turn the cardboard pieces over so they remain 1/4" apart. Tape them with duct tape, maintaining that 1/4" gap. Turn the card-board back again. Lay another piece of duct tape on this side. Press down between the two pieces of cardboard, so the two sides of tape adhere

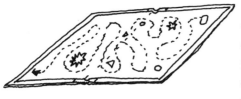

to each other in the gap. Now you have a strong hinge.

Meanwhile, draw the game board on another sheet of paper. It should be almost as big as the opened cardboard. (If there is about a 1/4" margin around the edge, it is less likely to get dog-eared with use.) Glue the game onto the cardboard, right over the duct tape hinge. Now you should be able to fold the board shut with the game on the inside.

Musical Fun

When you and your children sing, they can accompany the songs with their own rhythmic instruments!

Maracas: Save burned out light bulbs for this project. Cover a light bulb with paper mache. Be sure to cover it with many layers so it will be sturdy when dry. After it is dry, bang it on a table until the glass inside breaks. The pieces will rattle inside the paper mache covering. Paint the maracas and give them a clear protective coating.

Tube Rattles: Take a cardboard tube - from a toilet paper or paper towel roll - and attach paper with masking tape to one end to close it. Put dried beans, rice, lentils or corn inside (the sound will vary with each) and cover the open end with more paper and masking tape. Cover the entire rattle with layer after layer of paper mache. When it is dry, paint it and give it a protective coating. (You can also decorate it with feathers, crepe paper streamers, gift wrap ribbons...)

Paper Plate Rattles: Flatten a cardboard tube (paper towel or toilet paper tube) and put one end between two small paper plates. Staple it in position. Staple the plates together all around, leaving a small opening. Pour dried beans into the opening, and staple that shut. Decorate the plates and handle with crayon, marker, yarn, feathers, crepe paper streamers....

Tip:

At a birthday party for young children, put them to work making rattles, and then let them shake them and dance their wiggles away in a lively parade.

Communications

We all have a need to record, to express, to share our meaningful moments, private epiphanies and personal passages. And we and our children can learn to create our personal talismans ourselves. Words of inspiration, of humor, of poetry, can be hand lettered in a piece of artwork and framed. Memories of a special visit, a cherished place, a special vacation, can be captured in a souvenir art work. Personal diaries, travel journals and collections of personal writing are even more inspiring when the books themselves are hand crafted by the writer. All of these forms of personal communication are endowed with even more meaning when our children can learn to make them for themselves and to share with others.

Souvenirs

A family driving trip through the southwest, a visit to Washington DC, a camping trip to a beautiful mountain lake...we try to keep these pleasures fresh in our memories with souvenirs. But these don't have to be store-bought... we can make them ourselves.

Sometimes we want to share our memories. Tokens of home to send to an older sibling away at college. Private recollections to share with a sweetheart. These can be made as gifts of memory.

Memory Collage: After a trip, make a collage of the little things that collect in pockets and suitcases...ticket stubs, maps, menus, notes...add snapshots, and commentary if you like. After a camping trip make a collage of leaves, pressed flowers, small twigs and tiny pebbles. Write the date and the place name.

Personalized Map: Draw a map of a trip, drawing pictures of special places, special times. Add snapshots and other memorabilia if you like.

Clearly Remembered: Using the clear plastic available in fabric stores, sew a pocket, put memorabilia in it, and sew it shut.

Pressed Flowers: A few flowers to remember a special place can be pressed and then mounted on paper (black, white or colored.) A lovely touch is to use a metallic gold marker to write the date and the place name. Then frame it. What a lovely remembrance, and what a lovely gift to send to Grandma after a visit!

Treasure Boxes

    Everyone has something precious to keep...shells, rocks, baseball cards, marbles, buttons and beads, paper dolls, photos... A special collection deserves a special container.

Tin Canisters: Take a can with a lid...coffee cans and tea canisters will do but cookie tins are ideal because they are often in more useful shapes. Shallow squares, rounds or rectangles are the easiest for treasure storage and retrieval. Paint it with white primer. Paint pictures or a design on it. When it is dry, give it a protective top coat.

Memory Box: Keepsakes (or travel snapshots) can rest in a decorated box...Start with a sturdy box with a good lid. If it does not have an attractive background color, paint it with white primer. Decorate it with a collage of gift wrap, wallpaper, cut out pictures, photos, perhaps with memorabilia (tickets, maps, notes, an autograph...). If you are making this treasure box as a gift for someone, try to think of what kinds of colors and patterns that person would like. You can also decorate the box with fabrics, laces, ribbons, decorative cord, sequins...

One of a Kind Posters

The poster, whether it be a wise proverb or a humorous quote, a political statement or a tribute to a hero, can be a deeply satisfying thing to make.

Teenagers especially love this art form. They are just beginning to be aware of their beliefs and to flex their own opinions. They live in a sometimes wild and wacky non-adult world that needs expression and outlets. They are starting to buy their own posters to express their attitudes, but making their own wall art is a much more powerful and meaningful release for this need.

Younger children too like to make a statement, although it is usually more benign. An eight year old will get a lot of pleasure out of making a sign that says *Art is Forever* or *I Love Rainbows*.

Lettering can be directly painted or drawn, typed on a separate sheet and glued on, stenciled, printed with stamps, assembled from words and letters cut out from magazines *(see page 116)* or spelled out with rubdown vinyl letters *(see page 64)*.

Quotation Art: Combine words with the visual elements of color and design. You can illustrate the words, or create a completely abstract work of colors and shapes around the words. The words can be written in pencil, traced over in pen, a black marker, or paints, and the art can be done around them.

Younger children will find this easier to grasp if they work with a single word or, at most, just a few words. An older child can work with a much longer quote. Also, young children like to plunge right in but older children may want to work out a rough copy to plan the layout of the words and visuals.

Pastels are very effective when combined with words. They lend themselves to abstract treatments, and they can completely cover the page with color without obliterating words.

Finally, for an effect similar to Medieval illuminated manuscripts, try enhancing your lettering with gold metallic markers.

Framing Tip

One way to get around the high cost of framing is to buy inexpensive dime store frames. Unfortunately, these are usually not as fine as the art that goes in them. One solution? You can paint them. Even the cheap metal frames can look much better painted white.

Spray them with primer first and then choose a finish color. You may want to have fun, painting them creatively to make as much of a statement as the art within them...with zebra stripes, or red and purple checks, green and pink paint spatters, or black sponge prints on bright colors...

"Ransom Note" Poster: A magazine cut-out collage can create a poster that is quirky and fun. The individual letters, or entire words, can be cut from magazine headlines, for a "ransom note" look. Pictures can be cut apart and manipulated to illustrate it.

That Special Song: An original composition, a cherished piece of music, or a romantic song...one way to acknowledge it is to display it! Hand print the music and decorate it...illuminate it like an old manuscript, or do a collage around it that expresses its content.

Honoring an Idol: A budding young ice skater honors an Olympic Gold Winner...a young drummer knows "everything" there is to know about a famous jazz musician...a shy teen looks up to a successful and gregarious sports figure...a "horse crazy" preteen collects clippings about a Triple Crown winner. A way to express this is to make a collage about that person (or animal, as it may be), with pictures, newspaper clippings, magazine headlines, autographed concert programs, whatever makes up a part of that person on the pinnacle.

Variation: Sometimes a *place* is venerated...A beach town in Florida, a lake in the High Sierra, a Greek Island, a home town...photos, magazine pictures, postcards, menus, coasters, newspaper clippings...these can make up a collage to honor that place.

One of a Kind Books

Anyone can make a book. Young children love to write books. (No one has told them they can't!) They not only write new stories, they love to write their own versions of their old favorites.

But there are many other reasons for making a book. A handmade book can be a personal diary, a journal of special thoughts, a trip journal, a collection of sayings, a collection of sketches.

A book can be the focus of a special interest. A place to put the pictures, the clippings, the autographs, the notes. A sports book for the avid football fan, a place to record all the statistics. Or a ballet book for the young dancer, a place to put the programs.

Binding Your Own Book...

There are many ways to bind your own book. Young children will try to experiment with their own binding inventions. It seems they just have to learn from experience that scotch tape binding doesn't work very well! But when they are ready, some of the simpler ways to make books are shown here.

As they grow older, they will become more and more interested in forms of binding that look "finished". Your older child may need your help, but will enjoy the results he gets when he makes a book cover as described in *Covering a Cover (page 120)*.

Binder Books: Preschoolers especially love to cut out magazine pictures that strike their fancy, such as pictures of particularly cute animals. They can collect these in a binder that they decorate themselves. Each picture can be glued to its own page, perhaps on a sheet of colored construction paper. The cover of the binder can be decorated using squeeze tube dimensional fabric paints (*page 42*) or with a collage of pictures protected by a piece of clear contact paper.

Accordion Fold Book: Fold a long piece of stiff paper in half several times (A) until it is folded down to the size you want for each panel. Press the folds to crease them. Unfold, and then refold it into a zig-zag fold (B).

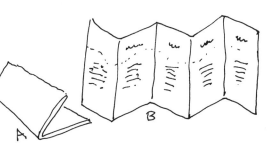

This is a lovely format for poetry. After the poems are copied into each panel (or written in one long line from panel to panel) the book can be folded up and tied with a silk cord, raffia, or special ribbon.

Variation: You can use heavy watercolor paper, and paint something (even just a light wash of colors) before you fold it. The words can be written after folding, over the watercolor wash.

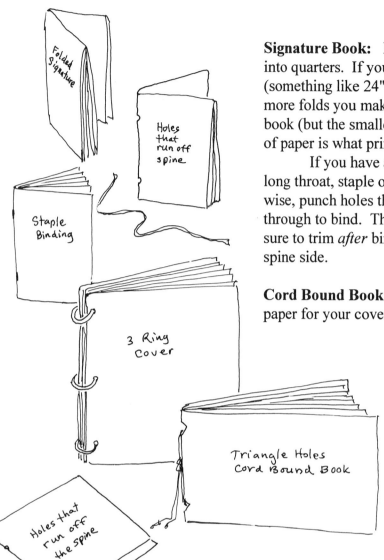

Signature Book: Fold a piece of paper in half, and then into quarters. If you start with a large piece of paper (something like 24"x30"), you can fold it many times. The more folds you make, the more pages you will have in your book (but the smaller each page will be). The folded sheet of paper is what printers call a signature.

If you have access to a stapler with an especially long throat, staple on the fold to bind your book. Otherwise, punch holes that run off the spine, and thread a cord through to bind. Then trim the top, bottom and sides. Be sure to trim *after* binding so you do not trim the bound spine side.

Cord Bound Book: You will need one sheet of heavy paper for your covers, some lighter paper for the inside pages of the book, and some cord to bind it (see the box for some ideas). Fold all the paper in half.

Punch holes in both sets of paper, letting the holes run off the spine. Or, cut triangles into the spine. Take the lighter weight paper and nest it, folded, inside the heavier paper cover. Line up both sets of holes. Thread cord through the two cuts so that the ends are on the outside, and tie.

A Three Ring Cover: Make two covers. Use a three hole punch to punch the covers and your inside pages. Reinforce the cover holes *(see facing page)*. Line up the inside paper in the covers and bind the book with binder-type metal rings (available in stationery stores).

A Hinged Cover: Prepare a hinged front cover and a straight back cover *(See Covering a Cover on page 120)*.

Cover your cardboard with patterned papers (wallpaper, gift wrap, marbled paper...), with fabric, or with a plain surface on which you mount a photo, a drawing, or a collage.

Make a title by printing it freehand, or use stencils or rub-down vinyl type.

Use a three hole punch to punch the covers and your inside

Ideas for Book Binding cord...

- ribbon
- raffia
- string (white, brown, colored)
- light rope
- silk cord, cotton cord
- leather thong
- gift wrap ribbon (curl the hanging ends)

pages, and reinforce the cover holes *(see below)*.

Line up the inside paper in the covers. Take about 4 feet of binding cord, and thread it in this order: through the top hole from front to back; through the middle hole from back to front; through the bottom hole from front to back; up the back and through the top to the front; through the middle again, from front to back; finally through the bottom hole to the front again. Tie the two ends together in the front, in a knot or bow, and trim the ends if they are too long.

Variation: Paint, draw, stencil or print a design on paper or fabric and use that to wrap the cardboard.

Laminated Art: Paint or draw a cover, including the title. Take it to a shop that does laminating and have it laminated *(see page 60)*. Punch holes and bind.

Handmade Paper: Make your *own* paper in the shape you want for a book cover *(see page 82)*. Be sure to make it with extra thick pulp. Because the tin can method usually makes a round piece of paper, make a round book! Cut your inside paper to a round shape to match. You may want to experiment with different kinds of cans to get square or rectangle shapes. Punch holes, reinforce the holes, and bind.

Spiral Bound: Prepare the inside pages and your covers, and then take your book to a copy shop where they can punch and bind it with a plastic comb spine (it is not really a spiral). These are inexpensive, fairly durable, and allow the book to open flat. Some shops will also offer true spiral binding, with a colored wire that spirals through the holes, but this is often a bit more expensive and can unwind at the top and bottom with a lot of use.

Tip:

Make your title on a separate piece of paper and glue it in place. This way if the first attempt does not turn out as you want it, you can simply make more, and choose the best to put on the book.

To Reinforce Holes

Punched holes will fray over time. You can reinforce them with eyelets if your cover material is sturdy enough.

Eyelets, originally intended for fabric use, are two piece metal caps that fit together (often with a tap of a hammer) to form a neat, strong metal-lined hole. Eyelet kits are available in several sizes, in the notions sections of fabric stores.

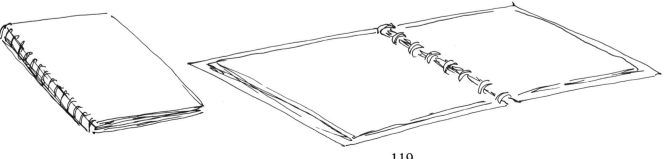

Covering a Cover

With this process, you make a hinged front cover out of light cardboard covered with decorative paper, and a matching back cover. This is a complicated process for young children, but very rewarding for the older ones.

Step 1: Cut your back cardboard cover to the size you want for your book. *Make a note of the measurements for Step 3.* Measure and cut a second piece of cardboard that is the same size as the first from top to bottom, but ¼" smaller from side to side. This smaller one will be the front.

Step 2: Set the back piece aside. Take the front piece and cut off a 1" strip along the spine. Line these two pieces up side-by-side about ¼" apart, and tack them together with masking tape (A). Turn the whole thing over (B) and lay a piece of duct tape on it, spanning the gap, overlapping both pieces (C). Turn the cover over again and remove the masking tape. Put a second piece of duct tape on this side, and press the two pieces of tape together in the gap (D). You now have a sturdy hinge for your front cover.

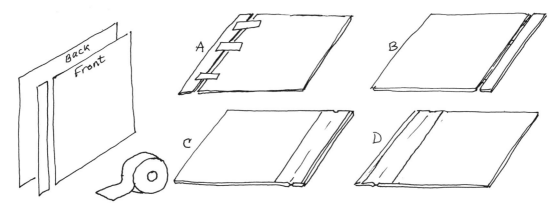

Step 3: Take your measurement from Step 1, and measure and cut your four pieces of cover paper (they do not all have to be the same pattern or color). Two pieces will be to cover the *outsides* of the cardboard covers. These will be 2" *bigger* than the cardboard on all four sides (or 4" bigger each dimension.) The other two pieces will be to cover the *insides* of the covers, and will be ¼" *smaller* than the cardboard on all four sides (or ½" smaller each dimension). Example: If the cardboard is 9" x 12", the outside cover papers will be 13" x 16", and the inside cover papers will be 8½" x 11½".

Step 4: Take one of your *outside* cover papers, wrong side up, and center one of the cardboard pieces on it. Make pencil marks in each corner, as shown at right with dots (A). Then cut the paper where marked with dashes (B). Do the same with your other outside paper.

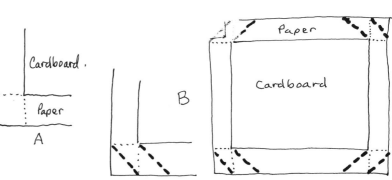

Covering a Cover, Continued

Step 5: Take the two outside cover papers that have been cut in Step 4, and apply adhesive to the wrong side of one of them. (Use spray mount or brush on white glue diluted with some water.) Place it in front of you, wrong side up, but with top and bottom correctly aligned. Center your *hinged* front cover on it, with the hinge side on the *right*. Turn the cover over, smoothing the paper in place. Make sure it follows the contours of the duct tape over the gap, so it will not crack later when the hinge opens and closes.

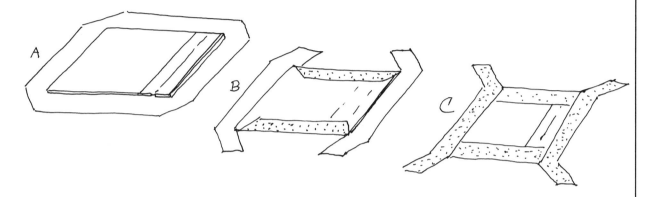

Step 6: Turn the cover over again. Fold the top and bottom flaps up and over the cardboard (B). If you used white glue, you may need to apply more to be sure they stick properly.

Step 7: Fold the side flaps over and onto the cardboard (C).

Step 8: Wrap the corner flaps around the corners so they form a triangle on the outside, and come around to finish inside (D through G).

Repeat for the back (unhinged) cover.

Step 9: Take your two inside cover papers, and apply your adhesive to one of them, and carefully center it on the uncovered side of the cardboard. It should overlap the flaps from the outside cover paper, and come to within 1/4" of the edge (H).

Repeat with second inside cover paper.

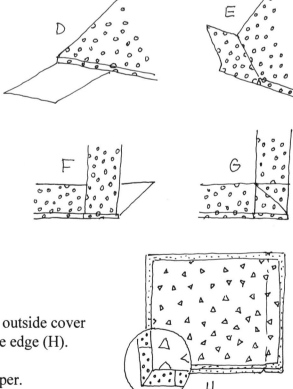

Gift Giving

Gifts made by hand are truly gifts from the heart. We want our children to learn to give with pleasure, and what greater pleasure than to *make* a gift for someone special? And what could be a more cherished gift than one made by a child? Children can make gifts, they can make the gift wrapping, they can make greeting cards. And encouraging them to do so affirms their worth and nourishes their creativity.

To Score Cardboard:

If you have ever tried to fold a piece of cardboard, you'll know that it's virtually impossible to get a straight, neat crease. *Scoring* cardboard prior to folding makes it possible to make a fold that is straight and placed exactly where you want it.

You'll need a ball-point pen that is out of ink. On the side of the cardboard that will be on the *outside* of the fold, run the pen along a ruler several times, pressing firmly to impress a straight mark where you want the fold to be.

 Then fold on that score line.

Presentations

Children love to make their own *packaging* for gifts. Encourage them to make the gift wrap for birthday gifts by drawing on a large piece of paper... butcher paper, drawing paper, tissue paper. Encourage them to make the card. And as they get older, they can make fancy boxes and bags.

Gift Bag: Have the child take apart a ready-made gift bag to see how it is made. Then use that as a pattern to make her own. It can be made of gift wrap, her own

painted paper, or fancy papers (handmade...metallics...
marbled...)

Gift Box: Have the child take apart a box to see how it is
made. Use that as a pattern for making his own box. After
assembling the box, use spray adhesive or diluted white
glue to cover it with decorative paper, use white glue to
attach a collage of papers, or prime it and paint it. Note:
When working with cardboard, you'll need to *score* the
folds before folding.

Greeting Cards

        Encourage your children to make their own
birthday cards instead of buying them. If you start this at an
early age, it will become a tradition, anticipated by all your
family members, and one that they may continue all their
lives. In addition to birthday cards, urge them to make all
kinds of greeting cards, and party invitations too.

One-of-a-Kind Special Cards

        Before starting any of these card ideas, choose your
format *(see page 125)* and prepare your paper.

Simply Drawn: With crayons, markers, colored pencils or
aquarelles, draw on the cover. Write the message inside
and perhaps draw inside as well. The envelope too can be
decorated with a colorful border or additional drawing.
*(Remember, if it is to be mailed, allow room for addressing
and stamping; the postal workers may appreciate the work
of art, but they will need to be able to read it.)*

Art in a Frame: Paint or draw a small
picture. Glue it onto a piece of colored or
decorative paper that is a bit bigger than the
picture, but not as big as the front of the card.
This is the "frame". Mount the "framed"
picture on the folded card and write a greeting
inside.

Fine Materials Collage: Make a tiny collage using handmade papers, origami papers, lace, doilies, ribbon, metallic twine, foils, small beads or shells, colored cellophane, or tissue papers. Or take scissors to a discarded painting, cutting it up into pieces; use the pieces as abstract components, chosen for their colors or lovely brush strokes. Choose a paper for the folded card that contrasts or blends with the collage colors. Mount the collage on this folded card and write a greeting inside.

Printed Pictures Collage: Use magazine picture cutouts, gift wrap papers, and recycled greeting cards to make a collage on the front of the folded card.

Stenciled Cards: Design a simple image and cut it out of heavy paper. You can have one large image that fills the front of the card, or a small image that gets repeated as a pattern. Lay the stencil over the prepared card and rub colored pencil, crayons, or markers back and forth over the opening. Mix colors generously for exciting effects. Or, dab with paint or inks.

Candy Card: Make a design that centers around a piece of wrapped candy glued onto the card.

Photo Card: Decorate a card with a picture of yourself, your family, your pets...whatever would be of interest to the person you are giving the card to! Draw a frame around the picture, draw an environment for the picture, or make a "continuation" of the picture *(see page 71)*.

Serial Card: This is a nice idea when you want to send a card to someone who is ill...turn one card into two, or more, and send them one after another. You can tell a story in two or more parts, or a riddle in one and the answer in the next. In the first card you can write *"To be continued in the next card"* or *"For the answer you'll have to wait for the next card!"*

Formats for Greeting Cards:

The following formats are for using standard 8½ x 11 sheets of paper and standard announcement or business sized envelopes. Announcement envelopes are available in stationery stores and often in art supply stores. Of course you can use other sizes and shapes...it just takes a little imagination!

FORMAT #1: Printed only one side and folded like a letter to go in a business size envelope.

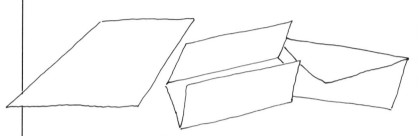

This is the easiest format for a small child to understand and work with. The entire 8½ x 11 sheet can be devoted to the picture, allowing some room for the written communication.

FORMAT #2: Printed only one side and folded to fit an announcement envelope:

Fold a sheet of 8½ x 11 paper in half (A), then fold into quarters (B). Hold it so the folds are on the left spine and on the top.

If you plan to use a photocopier to reproduce your cards, make a folded sample to work from. Write *Front* on the front cover, write *Inside Left* and *Inside Right* inside, and write *Back* on the back cover . Unfold the paper (C). You will notice that some of the words are upside down. This is your "blueprint" for setting up the card. *This can be confusing and frustrating for a small child, so using this style for photocopying should be avoided until a child is old enough to follow the format.*

FORMAT #3: Printed two sides, cut and folded to fit in an announcement envelope:

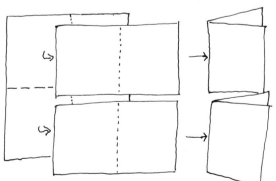

This works best on heavier paper or card (cover) stock. Take an 8½ x 11 sheet and cut it in half, to two 8½ x 5¼ sheets. You will have two cards to fold in half to be 5¼ x 4¼ . If your paper stock is stiff, be sure to score before you fold *(see page 122)*.

Pop-out Cards

Everyone loves pop-out cards. Once your child masters the mechanics of making them, they can be used in all kinds of imaginative ways. The pop-out can be a picture...an animal, a person, a car, a building. It can be a shape with words on it. It can be whatever you want it to be. Add a cover design and you've got an imaginative card!

Here are three easy versions, all based upon using Format #3 on page 125.

Pop-out Card #1

Cut a strip of heavy paper. Fold it in a zig-zag pattern. Glue one end of the strip to the inside of the card. Glue the figure or form that will pop out on the other end.

When the card is folded closed, you must be careful that the zig-zag strip is folded down into a "closed" accordion shape.

Pop-out Card #2:

1. Take two pieces of colored construction paper, both the same size and folded to the final size. One will be the card's inside, one will be the outside. (A)

2. Take the folded *inside* piece of paper *only*, and draw the pop-out shape very lightly in pencil on the fold (B). Cut it almost out, *leaving the bottom middle of it still attached to the fold (C).*

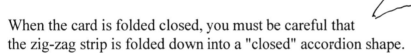

3. Glue the front and back sections together *without* gluing the pop-out image (D). Fold the unglued portion out, towards the sides when the card is folded closed.

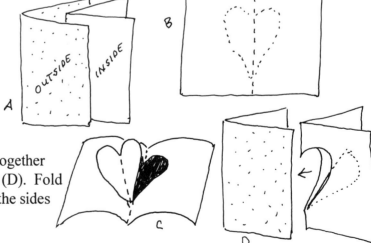

Pop-out Cards, Continued

Pop-out Card #3

1. Follow step 1 for Pop-out Card #2.

2. Take the folded *inside* piece of paper *only*,
    and make two parallel cuts, about an inch
    apart, and about halfway to the edge (A).

    The rectangle area formed by these two cuts
    will be the pop-out holder.

    Open the paper and fold it flat. Measure
    the width of the cuts (B).

3. On a third piece of paper design a simple shape
    and cut it out. The easiest way for younger kids
    to do this is to fold the paper in half and cut out
    the shape on the fold as shown in the stencil cutting
    tip on page 87. Be sure that this shape is exactly
    as wide as the width of the parallel cuts. This is
    what will "pop out" (C).

4. Glue the front and back sections together *without
    gluing the pop-out holder between the two cuts.*
    Fold the unglued portion out away from the card
    (towards the sides when the card is folded.) (D)

5   Fold the cutout, wrong sides together, and glue the
    cutout to the center unglued portion. (E) Be sure
    that when the card closes the pop-out is properly folded.

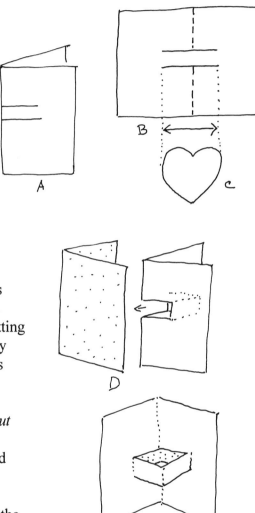

Cards in Quantity

Note cards left blank inside make lovely gifts when they are bundled with coordinating envelopes and tied with a piece of raffia or ribbon. As with the One-of-a-Kind cards, decide on your format and have your paper already prepared in advance. (Sets of blank note cards and envelopes in various fine papers are available in some stationery stores and in many art supply stores.) Refer to the sections about printing materials *(pages 56 to 59)* and duplicating an image *(pages 84-89)*.

Rubbing: Cut out pieces of cardboard into interesting shapes. Glue them onto another piece of cardboard in a pleasing design. Lay each card cover over the cardboard, and rub with a crayon.

Stamping : Use potato stamps, sponge stamps, gadgets, or even stamps made from fired modeling clay. Stamp the image into patterns, or in a random design.

Printing: Linoleum blocks and wood blocks allow you to make large numbers of cards with the same image. You can do more than one color at a time by applying two colors onto the block before laying the paper on it. Older children can even do more than one color in succession if they understand how to keep it all in registration *(see page 86)*.

Xerox Printing: If you create your original in black and white (preferably in pen because pencil will not reproduce well), you can have your design duplicated by a copy machine. They can then be hand-colored, if desired. Many copy shops have a wide range of papers available, including heavier cover stock and fine rag paper.

School Valentines:

Every year many classrooms have a valentine exchange. This year, instead of buying the season's mass-produced punch-out cards, try some of the following ideas for making something more personal (but still manageable in large quantities). Of course any of these ideas can be the basis of a far more elaborate valentine for someone special!

As these are exchanged in the classroom, they do not need to be standard mailing sizes. Smaller sizes make it easier to make a large quantity. Cut heavy drawing paper into the number of cards you need, big enough to fold in half if desired.

Potato Stamp Valentines: Cut a potato in half, carve a heart shape on the cut end, and cut away the background. Use a red stamp pad or pour some paint onto a paper plate. Stamp the prepared cards with the potato heart stamp dipped into the paint or on the stamp pad. A gold metallic marker is an elegant way to embellish and sign them.

Heart Stencil Cards: Draw a heart on a piece of heavy paper and cut it out. Be sure it is not too big to fit on the cover of the cards! Lay this stencil on one of the prepared cards. Holding it in place with one hand, rub colored pencils or crayons back and forth over the stencil opening. Experiment with many colors mixed together, and over each other. Smaller images are easier, and allow you to stencil more than one image on each card (but don't get carried away...remember that the more you do the longer it will take, and you are making cards for the entire classroom!)

Heart Rubbings: Cut out some cardboard hearts and glue them to a piece of cardboard that is about the same size as your valentine cards. Place each blank card over the cardboard and rub with crayon.

Mini Collages: Cut out heart shapes from construction paper in all sizes and colors. Prepare the cards by cutting heavy drawing paper into the desired number of cards, allowing for them to fold in half if desired. Glue the various cutout hearts onto the cards. You can also add other decorations if desired...snippets of lace, doilies, buttons, glitter, sequins, foil, stickers...or a piece of wrapped candy!

Cookie Valentines: Bake your favorite cutout cookies, using a heart cookie cutter. For very young children, lay all the cookies in a tray and let them squiggle cake decorating gel over them (you buy these in tubes in grocery stores). Older children may want to "paint" with frosting. Prepare your favorite icing, color it with food colors and thin it with water. Paint it on the cookie with a clean (preferably new!) paintbrush. Package the cookies in plastic sandwich bags, with a cutout heart or heart-shaped doily for the "to and from" names.

Birthday Party Invitations

Rather than buy ready-made invitations, you can have your child make them easily at home. You can use any of the Valentine ideas, or you can try "Xerox Printing".

Xerox Printing Invitations: Refer to Formats #1 and #2 on page 125. Choose a format and then have your child draw a party picture. It should be done in black ink so that it copies well. You can have this photocopied onto white or colored paper, and then she can decorate it with colored pencils, markers or crayons.

Making Gifts

Children can make lovely gifts for birthday and holiday giving. By making a gift instead of buying it, a child is truly participating in the experience. Of course, many of the ideas on these pages are things a child may want to make for herself.

Book Marks

Book marks are a simple gift for children to make, and they are always useful!

Book Creatures: On card stock, heavy drawing paper or heavy construction paper, draw a creature's outline...an animal, a person, a smiling sun...it should be long and thin, about bookmark size, or smaller to be attached to the top of a bookmark. Color it and cut it out. If it is a small shape, glue it onto a long piece of paper... perhaps in a contrasting color.

Laminated: On a strip of paper about 1¹/₂" wide, paint or draw a design. (It is fun to incorporate the recipient's name.) Or you can draw several bookmarks on one sheet, laminated them as one, and then cut them apart later. To get them laminated you have to take them to a shop that offers this service *(see page 60.)*

Leather with Gold or Silver: If you have access to leather scraps, this is an elegant gift for a child to make. Cut a piece of leather into a strip. Using a gold or silver metallic marker draw a design on the piece of leather. You can cut the bottom end into a fringe.

Clear Message Book Mark: Using clear plastic from a fabric store, sew two strips together on three sides, leaving one end open. Drop in confetti (available in heart shapes, dollar signs, and palm trees, just to mention a few), a fortune from a fortune cookie, a picture, cut out shapes, little notes...as long as each insert is flat, your imagination is the only limit for personalizing this book mark. Then sew the end shut.

Personal Treasures

Clay Bead Necklace: Use oven fired clay to make beads *(see page 103).* Vary the sizes, shapes and colors. Experiment with different bead stringing patterns (*See About Patterns, page 88,* and look at other necklaces for pattern ideas.) Don't try to make too many beads - a small number on a leather thong or silk cord can be very effective, and much easier for a child to handle. Fire them and paint them, if the clay is not colored. Experiment by combining colors on the beads. Give them a clear glossy coating. String them on a piece of silk cord or leather thong.

Paper Triangle Pin: Using wall paper scraps, Origami paper, homemade paper, or scraps from watercolor brush stroke practice, cut pieces into triangles and stack them different ways. When they look just right, glue them together. When dry, brush with decoupage glue. When that dries, glue a pin-back on the back. (You can try other shapes too.)

Clay Barrette: Take a barrette backing (available in craft stores) and measure it. Make a shape out of oven-dried clay that is slightly bigger than the backing. Fire it, paint it (if it isn't colored clay) and give it a clear finish. Then glue it to the barrette backing.

Pretty Stuff Barrette: Take a barrette backing and glue on a big bow, or ribbons, beads, shells, buttons...

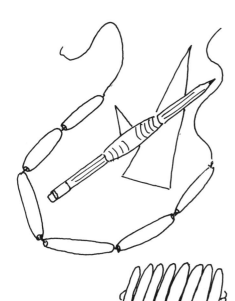

Magazine Beads: Cut a brightly colored magazine page into triangles. Roll the triangles up around a pencil, starting at the wide end. Glue the pointed end down. When the glue dries, gently slide the bead from the pencil. String onto cord or yarn to make a necklace. If you want a smaller center hole, roll the beads on bamboo cooking skewers. Experiment with triangles of different sizes and shapes.

Variation: Line up short magazine beads on a barrette backing, glue them in place and brush with decoupage glue.

Personalized Tote Bag or Backpack: Start with a plain-colored tote bag or backpack. These can sometimes be found in white muslin in craft stores. Decorate with fabric paints. You may need to stuff the bag with towels when you apply a hot iron to set the paints.

Decorated T-shirt: Paint a plain T-shirt with fabric paints. This is easier if you slip a piece of cardboard inside it, big enough to stretch it flat.

Dyed Silk Scarf or Tie: Craft stores that specialize in textile crafts often carry silk paints, white silk scarves and men's ties. Follow their directions carefully. Use silk paints rather than dyes - easier for kids and inexperienced adults!

Household Things

Juice Lid Magnet: On a frozen concentrate juice lid, make a collage...of ribbons and lace...dried beans...cutout pictures...or glue on a tiny painting. Spray with a clear finish, or brush on a decoupage glue. Glue a magnet piece on the back (available in craft stores). If the magnet piece is small, glue several so that the magnet holds its own weight in addition to a paper or two without slipping.

Clay or Dough Magnets: Make a small shape in air-dried or oven-dried clay. Dry or fire it, paint it, give it a clear glossy protective coat, and then glue a magnet piece (or several) to its back.

Clothespin Magnets: Paint a wooden clothespin with a colorful design... stripes, dots, spatters...Give it a face, perhaps with movable eyes! Finish with a protective glossy coat. Then glue several magnet pieces to its back.

Coasters: Paint or draw designs on small squares of stiff white cardboard. Laminate or cover with clear contact paper.

Fabric Placemats: Cut out and hem four (or more) pieces of solid color fabric, all the same size (which should be big enough to be a useful placemat after hemming.) Use fabric paints to decorate. Be sure to iron the fabric paints after they dry, to set them.

Laminated Placemats: Paint or draw on four pieces of placemat-sized paper, all the same size. Then take them to a shop that does laminating *(see page 60)*.

Ornament: Using a glue gun, cover a Styrofoam sphere by gluing on tiny pinecones or dried beans. Tie ribbons around it, securing them with pins, to form a loop at the top for hanging.

Variation: Paint it gold.

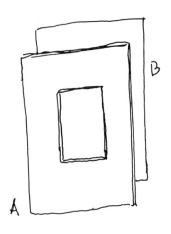

Picture Frame: This is a special way to frame a photo. Take a pre-cut mat board with an opening already cut out for a picture (A). These are available in frame shops and art supply stores. Cut a piece of cardboard to the same outside dimensions, to be the picture backing (B). Cut another piece of cardboard into the shape shown, score it and fold it (C). Attach the folded part of the triangle (C) to the cardboard backing (B) to be the picture support (D). Be sure you attach it so the large end is at the bottom.

Decorate the front piece (A). You can paint it. You can glue tiny pinecones, dried beans, or small sea shells on it. Or you can make a collage on it with beautiful papers, fabrics, lace...

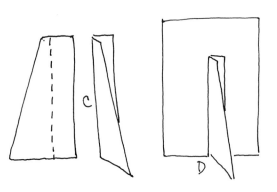

When the front (A) is dry, carefully turn it over and tape the photo or artwork into place, face side down. (If you wish, you can cut a piece of clear acetate to act as glass, taping it into place over the opening, *before* you put the photo in place.)

Attach front and back (E) with two-sided tape (scotch tape that is sticky on both sides).

Variation: Glue on macaroni of all shapes, and paint with gold paint before Step E.

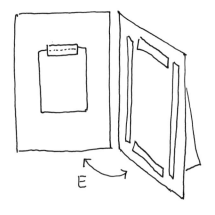

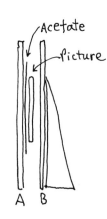

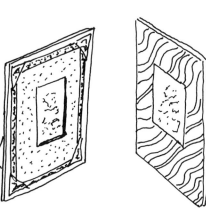

Garden Art:

There are lovely things from the garden that both inspire a child's creativity and make beautiful gifts.

Vine Wreaths: If you have honeysuckle or wisteria vines, you are in luck. These vines are so small and supple they are easy for a small child to wind onto a form. If they are at all stiff, soak them in water first.

Take a block of wood (about 6" square) and draw a circle in pencil. Hammer finishing nails (the ones without heads) into the wood along the circle shape. Space the nails about 1" apart.

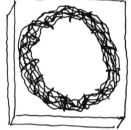

Take some cuttings and strip them of their leaves. Wind the vine around the nails of the circle shape, going outside one, inside the next, outside again, and so on. When you reach the end of the strand, tuck it under and start with the next strand. This next one should be the opposite of the first...inside where the first was outside, outside where the first was inside. Make the wreath as thick as you wish (or as thick as the child can stay interested.) A final strand then winds around and around all the others.

Keep the wreath on its form for at least a week, and then lift off. Wire on bows, herbs, and dried flowers.

Variation: Make the form into a heart shape.

Hanging Sprig: Wire together sprigs of herbs and dried flowers. They can be decorated with cinnamon sticks, bundled, and tied with ribbon. Tie a bow at the top. If you use wired ribbon the ends can be formed into pretty shapes. (This ribbon is available at some fabric stores and craft stores.)

Painted Pots: Treat terra-cotta pots (clean new ones) with wood sealer on the inside. This will help prevent the water from seeping through to discolor your painted side. Paint the outside

with acrylic paints, either directly on the terra-cotta, or with a white base coat and bright colors over that. Older children may want to plan their design before starting. Younger children will usually want to work free-form.

Variation: Make a matched set as a gift...a set of three in different sizes, or two the same size.

Variation: Plant herbs, lettuce, flowers, or bulbs in the pots as a gift.

Lettuce Garden, Herb Garden: Plant lettuce seeds, or herbs such as basil or parsley, in a planter (a pulp pot is a very inexpensive alternative to the high cost of a ceramic or wooden planter). Measure the top, and cut a piece of heavy paper (or light cardboard) the same size as the top. On this paper, draw a picture of what is planted, and perhaps pictures of food prepared with the plant. Write out any appropriate instructions, and perhaps include a recipe or two. Lay the finished drawing on the top of the planter and tie it with a ribbon. (You will want to wait until the last minute to put the paper over the planter, as it will interfere with watering the seeds.)

Variation: Plant flowering bulbs instead of seeds.

The artist finds
greater pleasure in painting
than in having completed the picture.

Seneca

Appendix

Basic Supplies

Try to Have:
crayons
markers
watercolor paints
brushes
white glue
paste
scotch tape
masking tape
scissors
ruler
construction paper
newsprint
drawing paper
stapler
recycled materials (*see right*)

Nice to Have:
watercolor paper
colored pencils
tempera paints
metallic markers
fabric paints

Useful to Have:
hole punch
glue gun
duct tape
jewelry pliers
white primer paint

Recycled Materials:
frozen concentrate lids
bottle caps
corks
boxes
cookie tins
styrofoam
little jars
film containers
gift wrap
ribbon
fabric scraps
fabric trims
yarn
string
thread spools

Found Things
shells
twigs
driftwood
pebbles
feathers
pinecones

Resources

Your best source of materials, technical information, and classes in your community will be your local art and craft supply stores. However, if you live where these are not available, there are some mail order sources. Call for catalogs.

Amaco
800/374-1600
(Clay products, tools, equipment & books for all kinds of clays)

Chaselle
800/242-7355
(Broad range of art & craft supplies

Dharma Trading Company
800/542-5227
(Fabric painting & dying supplies)

Graphik Dimensions, Ltd.
800/221-0262
(Framing materials)

Janet Coles Beads
800/232-3269
(Beads & jewelry supplies)

Nasco
800/558-9595
(Broad range of art & craft supplies)

Utrecht
800/223-9132
(Painting & drawing materials)

Gift Ideas

Give a child yet another toy and it will soon be broken or forgotten. But give art materials and the child will put them to use for hours of enjoyment, and may even discover a new direction!

These ideas are just for starters. You'll get many more as you browse your art supply store.

For the very young...

- Collage materials: sequins, feathers, and beads; foam core squares; an assortment of papers (construction paper, tissue paper, metallics, cellophanes)
- A large crayon or marker set in a case
- Glitter crayons
- A blank T-shirt, and a set of dimensional squeeze tube fabric paints
- Assorted beads, with elastic and silk cord for stringing them

For all ages...

- Papers...construction paper, tissue papers, bright metallics and cellophanes, patterned origami papers, marbled paper, one-of-a-kind hand made papers
- A set of blank note cards with envelopes
- An age appropriate jewelry making kit
- A set of oven hardening clays in assorted colors
- A set of watercolors, good brushes, and some watercolor paper.
- A set of aquarelles and a pad of watercolor paper
- A blank sketch book
- A set of gold and silver metallic markers
- Fabric paints and a plain white muslin tote bag
- Jewelry pliers, assorted jewelry findings, a beading board, beads, and a gift certificate for more beads
- Glossy acrylic paints, and gold metallic paint
- Vinyl lettering
- Paper making kit
- Tie dye kit
- A clock mechanism
- A sewing machine

For the older crowd...

- A set of oil paints, palette, palette knife, turpentine and linseed oil
- Linoleum blocks, inks, brayer, cutters, and fine heavy printing paper
- A set of technical pens
- A calligraphy starter set
- A camera, film, a gift certificate for enlargements, some gallery frames
- Silk paints, guttas, and white silk scarves

And what to avoid...

Coloring books, paint by numbers, pre-made molds for modeling materials...

INDEX

Can art
be an *everyday thing*
for someone else
you know?

Order **Everyday Art for Kids**, and give it as a thoughtful gift to your friends and their families. Give it as a useful reference to grandparents, to day care providers, to teachers...to *anyone* who spends time working with kids, anyone who is looking for creative projects.

Please send me _____ copies of *Everyday Art* for Kids, @ $18 each _____

Handling _____ $.50

Order Total _____

Sales Tax_____

Postage (*See box*) _____

Total Enclosed_____

Postage (Book Rate)	
1 Book: $1.74	4 Books: $3.24
2 Books: $2.24	5 Books: $3.74
3 Books: $2.74	6 Books: $4.24

Please make your check or money order payable to Mockingbird Press.

Mockingbird  **Press**

PO Box 331, El Cerrito, CA 94530 510/528-7804